Love Like Jesus

The Ministry of Jesus, Volume 3

William F Johnson

Published by Aslan Press, 2020.

Love Like Jesus

The Ministry of Jesus, Volume 3
by
William F Johnson
Published by Aslan Press, 2020.

While every precaution has been taken in the preparation of this book, the publisher assumes no responsibility for errors or omissions, or for damages resulting from the use of the information contained herein.

LOVE LIKE JESUS

First edition. December 7, 2020.

Copyright © 2020 William F Johnson.

Written by William F Johnson.

http://**aslanpress.com**[1]

All rights reserved.

---

1. http://aslanpress.com

.

Acknowledgements

Writing a book is a solitary activity, but the content of the book is the result of hundreds of people who influence the life of the author, from which much of the material is often drawn. Those people would include spouse, parents, grandparents, siblings, friends, church families and business associates.

Specifically I want to acknowledge, Ron and Rebecca Bounds, Beth Wynn, Randall Neely, Martha Barton, Mike Norcon, Mark Probst, and Fr George Eber of St. Antony Orthodox Christian Church, Tulsa, for their friendship, helpful input, and support along the way.

Dedication

I dedicate this book to my wife Rita, our children - Kevin and Rhonda, and all of those who loved me despite myself. Without you all, there would be no book about love.

Introduction

"Love Like Jesus" is the third book in the series, "The Ministry of Jesus." This series of books was created to challenge the reader to become a disciple of Jesus Christ, by learning from Jesus, being equipped by Jesus, and following His call to continue His ministry in the world.

The Greek word translated "disciple," in most English bibles, is mathetes (Mathetes). A mathetes was an individual who attached him or herself to a master to learn and become like the master. Today, we call them apprentices and it is a proven way to develop master electricians, plumbers, and carpenters.

The role of a disciple of Jesus Christ is to become an apprentice to the Master, Jesus.

St. Paul could tell his followers in Corinth, "*Imitate me as I imitate Christ.*[1]"

It is too bad we all cannot say that. We fall short of truly imitating Christ. However, as we search the scriptures, we see Jesus and are able to imitate His example as described by those who knew Him best, Matthew, Mark, Luke, and John.

Bill Johnson

Chapter 1 - Facing a Crisis

We all face crises our lives. It is not a matter of "if," it is a matter of "when."

A crisis is a time of intense difficulty, trouble, and danger, or a time to make difficult or important decisions.

There will be several crises in a person's life. When one occurs in middle age, it is often called a "midlife crisis," a term coined by Canadian Psychologist Elliott Jacques in 1965. While modern research has shown that this is not a phase that most middle-aged people experience, it remains a common excuse for strange behavior.

Each major crisis is an opportunity to change life's direction. Change is scary because it can lead one into the unknown, where we must forfeit control. On the other hand, maintaining a life without change is comfortable and feels safe. Change feels reckless and unnatural as we abandon the common and reach out for something new. Only the adventuresome view change as exhilarating, the rest of us avoid that adrenaline rush.

My major crisis came just before I turned forty. Unhappy with the status quo, our family made major changes. After almost twenty years of dedicated service with a medium-sized electronics firm, I resigned, and we moved from the hustle and bustle of the nation's capital to the sleepy Mississippi Gulf Coast town of Pascagoula. Once a busy executive, now a senior engineer with a major defense contractor. No longer a frequent flier, I slept in my own bed and was home most of the time with my wife, teenage daughter, and young son. Overnight trips were rare. Gone were the weeklong trips to Los Angeles, New York, Boston, or Miami. It was a positive change, but not without problems, as we all had to adjust to the new family dynamics. Despite this, my workdays were challenging but calm, and for the first time in our married life, we attended church together as a family. Life was good and getting better.

But, deep down inside of me, I sensed something important was missing.

What was it? What was missing? I had no clue. It was as if I was an actor playing a part on the stage of my life. Nothing seemed real. My life was a theatrical production. I was empty.

That is when things became crazy. It had to have been God. Who else could manipulate world-wide geopolitical events to come together in such a way as to provide the opportunity for another major step in my spiritual life?

For over a month, Rita and I planned on attending a weeklong Christian conference in Atlanta in early June. Vacation was scheduled, hotel reservations made, and the travel itinerary set. We were to leave Pascagoula on Saturday, drop the kids off with family in Jackson, and then on Sunday, drive to Atlanta, for the conference to begin Monday.

On Tuesday, the week before we were to leave, everything fell apart. My vacation was canceled, and my boss informed me I was to fly to Los Angeles on Sunday for an urgent meeting regarding a contract we were working on for the Shah of Iran.

I panicked, the conference in Atlanta was an important step in our relationship with God which had become our top priority. Over the past year, we had both become serious about our faith and we were growing deeper in our Christian walk. But, I still had to earn a living.

For the next few days, we tried to figure out how we could salvage something out of our situation. Could Rita ride to Atlanta with someone else? Could I fly from Los Angeles to Atlanta after my meeting, in time to attend part of the conference?

On Thursday, the world received the news of the overthrow of the Shah of Iran. As a result, our contract and my Los Angeles meeting were postponed, and on Sunday, we headed to Atlanta for the conference that turned our lives in a new direction.

But that was not the crisis. The crisis came two weeks later.

After our return from the Atlanta meeting, that sense of emptiness became even stronger - something was still seriously missing in my life.

The conference was great and gave us direction, but it left me with many questions about myself and about God. That empty feeling kept growing.

On a hot Sunday morning, late in in June, Pastor Nick's sermon ran long, and he did not finish in the morning service. Apologizing, he told us he would finish it in the evening service. To this day, I do not remember the point of his message - it had something to do with love. But, while Nick was preaching, a spotlight lit up something in my mind. Stunned by the clarity of the insight, and realizing my brokenness, I feared what it meant to our future. At almost forty years of age, married to a loving wife and father of two fine children, I realized that I was devoid of the most rudimentary virtue of human life, love.

I lacked the ability to give and receive love.

Someone growing up in a dysfunctional family does not know that it is dysfunctional. It just seems normal because you do not know any better. Alcoholism, abuse, and rejection are often identifiable issues of dysfunction, but to those inside, they are only normal.

My family all called themselves Christian, but we did not attend church, and there were few examples of giving and receiving love.

I do not remember ever hearing the words, "I love you!" addressed to me or anyone else in the house which included three generations.

The evening service at our church in Pascagoula always ended with an opportunity to pray at the altar, an opportunity I mostly ignored. But that night, I was the first one down front.

Softly weeping, I knelt, and offered this desperate prayer: *"Lord, help me! Teach me to love."*

That was the crisis moment. I had to change but did not know how.

Since then, I found out that there are millions of people, just like me, who continue to suffer from an inability to give or receive love.

This was a major factor that motivated me to enter full-time ministry to help wounded people who need to know and understand the true and unfailing love of God.

Chapter 2 – Love, The Greatest Need

What a man desires is unfailing love; [Proverbs 19:22 (NIV)]
The greatest need of the Human heart is love. Receiving and giving love are the hallmarks of our humanity. If we are to be truly human, we must be able to love God, love ourselves, and love those around us with an unfailing love.

The problem is, we do not really understand what love is, nor do we know how to show our love properly to others. Too often our feeble attempts at love fail, and we are left alone, desolate, and discouraged.

There are millions of people in society who are unable to either give or receive love. I know because I was one of them and have met hundreds more just like me. Our world would be a different place if we all learned how to love.

Why is love so difficult? The following are several of the most important reasons we have noted.

Distorted view of Love: Because of each person's background and history, there is a distorted view of what love really means, and how to show love. It often seems that love has something to do with having our own needs met at the cost of another.

Lack of good role models: It may come as a surprise to you, but your parents and other family members were not perfect. They were, and continue to be, fallible human beings with their own problems. As a result, their love for us was inconsistent, often conditional, and at times missing.

Love is dangerous: Love requires a vulnerability to the object of our love, leaving us open to hurt and rejection. Rather than loving someone, we often avoid pain by avoiding love entirely.

Still, because of our great need, we continue our desperate search for a true love that will satisfy. When we do not find it, we substitute other things to fill our emptiness; career, drugs, alcohol, and/or unhealthy relationships. The results of these failed searches are found in prisons, hospitals, and rehab centers throughout the civilized world.

At times we may realize that our pursuit of love is little more than a vain attempt at finding security, and we are left alone to face our brokenness and accept that we will never find love. So, we give up trying. We isolate ourselves, still aching for a love that is real.

According to American psychologist Abraham Maslow,[3] a human being must first have four distinct levels of basic needs met before he or she can become a fully functioning human being.

Physiological needs are the first level of needs. We need food, shelter, and air to breathe.

The second level of needs is for **security** to be safe from harm.

After those two needs are provided, the next level of need for the human life is **love;** to be able to receive love and to be able to give love to others.

When those three levels of needs are satisfied, the person can develop **esteem,** which is the fourth level.

When the need for love is unfulfilled self-esteem is low and it is difficult for a person to love themselves and grow into their place in life. Humans have a need for a stable, firmly based high level of esteem, that is self-respect and respect from others, which is missing if love has not first been provided.

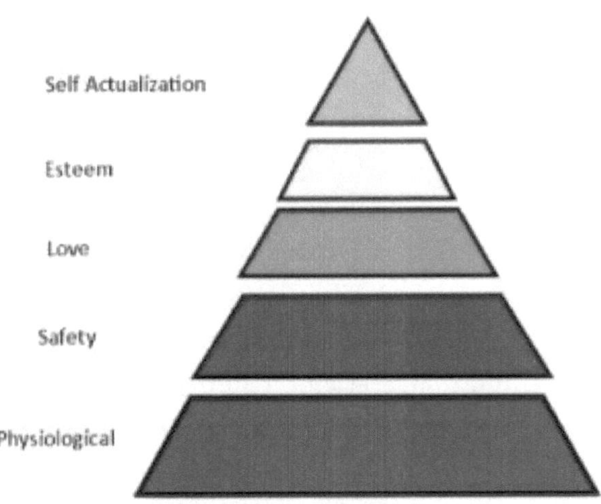

Around the world we see a growing lack of respect for peers, family, authority, home, and governments. Could the real problem be that the need for love has not been satisfied?

Only when the needs for sustenance, safety, love, and esteem are satisfied is the person ready for **self-actualization** or becoming the person for which, they were created to be.

Maslow describes self-actualization as a desire to be and do that which they were, "born to do." A musician must make music, an artist must paint, and a poet must write.

The ability to love and be loved stands directly in the path of our ability to live a satisfying life, and our ability to love others is rooted in our finding and being secure in receiving real, unfailing love.

We do not always realize our unmet need is for love, nor even that we have an unmet need. Unmet needs manifest themselves in a variety of physical, emotional, and spiritual ways, such as poor self-esteem, depression, misplaced anger, anxiety, abuse of alcohol and drugs, eating disorders, and other damaging activities. While these signs point to deep issues, people respond to them in different ways. Some over-medicate, others try to ignore the truth.

The absence of love leads to insecurity, and insecurity leads to a confused identity. Without identity we play a role in life trying to become whatever we believe others want us to be. As we bounce around, trying to please whoever we are near, we lose track of who we are. When playing a part, you are never free to be yourself. The relationships, we try so hard to cultivate, are broken when people realize our falseness. Broken relationships lead to more hurts, causing us to build protective walls. Walls keep us from becoming vulnerable but isolate us from anyone who would like to come in close.

When love is missing, everyone, children and adults, search to find something to fill their emptiness. Lacking any confidence, they wander around without purpose or identity, feel rejected, and doubt their own abilities. Their lovelessness leads to prodigal lifestyles - parties, alcohol, drugs, and immorality. Sex, drugs, and rock-and-roll lead to more emptiness and the reawakened desire to find love.

For some, broken patterns of addiction to sex, chemicals, work, or even religion, may develop. For others, it's can be an emotional or romantic ideal that they pursue in another which might lead to ties to abusive partners or unhealthy lifestyles. Some simply resign themselves to loneliness and mistrust. They give up on the hope of ever being loved. They become numb and cold, some married and some unmarried.

For young children, the source of love and security should be the immediate family, but when that family is dysfunctional, love may be missing or flawed. Those children grow up desperately searching for an unfailing source of love. Even in so-called "loving families," the love expressed is imperfect and often lacking in sincerity.

We must admit that our human sources of love usually disappoint. The love of a friend, parent, lover, brother or sister, or spouse, fails more often than it delivers. No human can love perfectly. Even when our human sources of love are strong, they are inadequate and will not fully satisfy our need for love nor provide us the fuel we need to love others properly. No one individual can bear the weight of our need for love.

Search me, O God, and know my heart; Try me and know my anxieties; [Psalm 139:23 (NKJV)]

As a child, it was poured into me that real men do not cry, so I stuffed my feelings, put on a happy face, and moved on. This attitude stayed with me for decades. After being hurt and rejected several times, I remember making a vow that I would never need anyone. "I can and would take care of myself."

I built this great wall around my heart to protect me from wounding. Unfortunately, that barrier kept me from receiving.

After graduating from college, it was - in my mind - a good time to get married, so I proposed to the girl I was dating, and she accepted. To this day, I remember an argument we had in which she angrily stated, "You don't need me!"

It was true. And I was pleased with that fact.

While in the army overseas, she finally had enough and left. My colonel called me in to offer some sage advice in dealing with my loss.

"In my experience," he said, "people respond in two equally destructive ways; they either drank too much or they bury themselves in their work."

His advice was heeded, but I was not able to decide what to do, so I found myself doing both. This self-destructive pattern continued even after leaving the service and re-entering the civilian world. I figured that hard work and long hours would encourage people to love me, while alcohol conquered my fear of rejection, enabling me to be outgoing and confident while seeking love. This combination provided a level of success in business, but my personal life kept getting worse.

Each of us has a desire to love others well in a way that contributes to the other's wellbeing as well as our own. To get there, we must face two things:

First, we must admit that we have been deceived and wounded by failed love. Since we are human, we are not perfect and often fail. Failed love can come down through generations.

Second, we must admit that, if we are to love freely, we need to be loved by an unfailing source of love, one that is deeper and truer than the human love we have experienced. We need Jesus and the love that is from above that can meet the needs of the deepest cries of our heart.

We human beings are like a sponge. When the sponge is dry, any water poured into it will be absorbed, until the sponge is saturated. When the sponge is full any new water flowing in will flow out. The only way we can genuinely love others is by being saturated with love. Not just any love will do. We need a source of love that is powerful and persistent. We need a source of love that is strong enough to break through our defensiveness and fear.

Chapter 3 - The First Step

And you shall love the Lord your God with all your heart, with all your soul, with all your mind, and with all your strength. [Mark 12:30 (NKJV)]

As I knelt at the altar, that Sunday evening in Pascagoula my prayer was answered. To this day, I don't know whether it was an audible voice, an overwhelming sense, or just an idea placed in my head, (choose your own theology), but God answered my prayer with these five words.

"First, you must love Jesus!"

The statement shocked and confused me. It did not make a lot of sense at the time, but I was desperate to try anything. Now, many decades later, I am still unpacking the meaning of the Lord's words.

Did I love Jesus?

I called myself a Christian. I was trying to follow Jesus, but did I love Him?

Probably not. After just at that moment realizing that I did not know much about love and did not know how to love; my guess is I did not love Jesus.

My father was right. When we children would begin to get overly proud of ourselves for something we did, he would respond with, *"Okay, but your feet stink and you don't love Jesus."*

"First, I must love Jesus," but how do I do that? I had recently read C. S. Lewis' book "<u>Mere Christianity</u>," and particularly the chapter on love. Lewis provides one answer as to how begin loving someone.

Lewis explains that if you want to love someone, but you do not have any warm feelings for them, you begin to do loving things for them.

He used the negative illustration of Adolf Hitler and the Jews during World War II, noting that Hitler hated the Jews. The more he hated them, the more he persecuted them, and the more he persecuted them, the more he hated them. As a result, Hitler and his followers tortured and slaughtered six million Jews in the Holocaust.

Lewis then illustrates how doing loving things instills loving feelings. The more loving things you do for someone, the more you will love them.

Still at the church altar, I remembered Lewis' advice and realized it could be used to answer my question, *"How do I love Jesus?"*

My first feeble attempt at loving Jesus was to just say to Him, *"Jesus, I love You!"* I repeated it over and over, *"Jesus, I love You. Jesus, I love You."*

Suddenly, my entire body became strangely warmed. It was as if I was being immersed in warm oil. It was the Holy Spirit. I have read of John Wesley's experience at Aldersgate Chapel, where his heart was strangely warmed during a Moravian meeting where Martin Luther's preface to the book of Romans was being read.

Now I knew what was missing in my life and had received the Lord's direction of how to repent, change direction. Psychologists will tell you that there can be a great gulf between realization and actualization. You may become cognizant of the need to change but change itself can be a difficult challenge. Realization can be instantaneous; but actualization can take a lifetime.

At the time, I wondered how loving Jesus could be the first step in loving my others.

Why was it important to first love Jesus?

When you love someone, you tend to become like them. If you love Jesus, you become like Him. Have you ever noticed how people who love one another for many years begin to look and act alike? A couple celebrating their golden wedding anniversary, not only act alike, but they even start to look alike in many aspects. You may have noticed similarities between pet-lovers and their treasures.

Great leaders are often followed by people who dress, act, and look like their idol. It is human nature to copy the things we most admire, people, pets, and idols.

We become like the gods we worship, whether our god is someone or something. It can even happen with a vocation or avocation.

When Jesus was asked to say which was the greatest commandment, without hesitation, He replied that we are to love God with all of our heart, mind, soul, and strength.[4] That represents a total commitment to love God with all of our being. As we grow in our love for God, we become more like Him.

Jesus is calling us into a deep relationship with God, and it comes at a time when most of us are not ready. We fear intimacy.

We spend our lifetime carefully building walls to protect ourselves from being hurt. Now, the Father's heart is calling us to break down our walls, walk with Him, and freely love Him with our full being.

It did not take long for me to realize that loving Jesus, or anyone else, requires much more than just saying a few words of devotion, no matter how well intentioned.

Saying the words, *"I love you,"* has become so overused in today's world that it has lost much of its power and meaning. Certainly, telling God you love Him is a valid first step, but it does not fulfill the scripture's call to love with all our heart, soul, mind, and strength.

Saint John, the Theologian, wrote, *"Let us not love in word or in tongue, but in deed and in truth.*[5]*"*

Chapter 4 What is Love?

"You know you're in love when you an't fall asleep because reality is finally better than your dreams." [Dr. Seuss]

For those of us that grew up with inadequate models of love, it is difficult to express love and even harder to accept that the love others offer us is unconditional. We desire a true, unfailing love where we do not have to manufacture a lovable persona. While we need and search for love, we do not even know for what we are searching.

The word "LOVE" is one of the most misunderstood and misused words in the English language. This simple, four letter word can bring joy, peace, conflict, heartbreak, and disaster.

Understanding what love is depends upon your history, culture, and vocabulary. Words are mere symbols - elements of language - used to communicate ideas. Communication is a two-way street. One person, the sender. wants to send a thought to another person, the receiver. When the connection works, the receiver understands what the sender means by his communication.

As a child, I was an avid radio listener and enjoyed the Western adventure series. One of my favorites was Tom Mix, a movie cowboy like Roy Rogers and Gene Autry. Tom Mix had a special offer for kids that encouraged us to listen every day. By sending in three box tops from packages of Ovaltine, Tom would send me my very own "secret code ring." With that ring, I could get his coded messages at the end of each program. Without the code ring, the message made no sense, but with my secret code ring I decoded every message.

All of us have our own secret code rings that we use when we communicate. The sender's thoughts are encoded as they pass from their mind to their mouth by a series of filters. The words, or actions, go to the receiver who must then interpret them. While the sender believes their thoughts are communicated accurately, the person on the receiving end may or may find an accurate understanding of the thoughts being communicated. The sender's words or actions must pass through the receiver's decoder. The accuracy of the communication is dependent upon both sender and receiver sharing similar code rings.

This may sound elementary, but if one looks at the political climate in the world today, you can see what happens when words and actions are misinterpreted. People seldom have the same code rings or filters. Filters are created through experience, knowledge, and traditions.

Someone who grew up in a Chicago ghetto, without a father, has a vastly different life experience than someone growing up in a comfortable suburban home with two loving parents. Their filters are totally different, they do not even speak the same language. The simple act of a gentleman opening the car door for a lady may become an utter disaster. The gentleman believes he is showing love by his actions, while an emancipated woman sees his actions as an insulting stereotypical action of a male chauvinist.

When you hear the word "love'" what images come to your mind? It all depends on your secret code ring, your filters.

When you hear the word dog, what images come into your mind? Some will see a cute puppy with a wagging tail, while another might be stricken with fear as they imagine an angry, vicious animal prepared to attack.

If we are honest, most of us think about love in terms of how it makes us feel. Writers of romantic songs, movies, and novels tend to define love in a way that involves getting our needs met or the mushy feelings such as a warm puppy, a chocolate sundae, or not having to say I'm sorry. They often look at love based upon what they can get out of relationship.

Behavior psychologist, Adam Grant identifies three fundamental styles of social interaction; "givers," "takers," and "matchers.[6]" Givers and takers are rare and sit at opposite ends of the social interaction spectrum. Matchers make up most of the population and often give to others based upon what they believe they will get in return. That is the way most of us view love, in terms of give and take.

If we are truly honest, most of us would define love in terms of getting our own needs met. Even generous acts of giving to others are often based upon an expectation of what we will receive in return. When offered attention, significance, or pleasure, we are eager to give, expecting that we will get something in return that we so desperately want or need.

But that is not love, that is selfishness and manipulation.

We even indoctrinate our children into believing they must earn love. Every Christmas season they hear the familiar story of "Rudolph the Red-Nosed Reindeer." If you remember the song written by Gene Autry, Rudolph was a tragic animal with a big, glowing, red nose causing him to be ostracized from the community. All the other animals laughed at him and called him names because of his appearance. That all changed when Santa needed him to guide his sleigh through a foggy Christmas eve. Then, after saving Christmas, Rudolph was loved by the other reindeer. They now loved him because he did something of significance.

Little children often have a better understanding of love. A group of psychologists delved into the meaning of love by asking a group of, four to eight-year-olds, what "love" meant. The children's answers were utterly amazing:

- "When my grandma got arthritis, she couldn't bend over and paint her toenails anymore. So, my grandpa does it for her now all the time, even when his hands got arthritis too. That's love..."
- "When someone loves you, the way they say your name is different. You just know that your name is safe in their mouths."
- "Love is when you go out to eat and give somebody most of your French fries without making them give you any of theirs."
- "Love is what makes you smile when you're tired."
- "Love is what's in the room with you at Christmas if you stop opening presents and listen."
- "If you want to learn to love better, you should start with a friend who you hate."
- "Love is when mommy gives daddy the best piece of chicken."
- "Love is when your puppy licks your face even after you left him alone all day."

- "When you love somebody, your eyelashes go up and down and little stars come out of you."
- "You really shouldn't say 'I LOVE YOU' unless you mean it. But if you mean it, you should say it a lot. People forget."

Love involves giving - giving beyond oneself. It means putting the needs of another ahead of our own. Love is the freedom to see beyond oneself to see another, not to see them as an object to meet your personal needs, but as one worthy of love.

A good definition of love is "Giving to someone beyond what one is getting in return."

At the time Christianity was beginning to spread throughout the Middle East the Apostle, Paul, writing to the church at Corinth offers a definition of love.

Love suffers long and is kind; love does not envy; love does not parade itself, is not puffed up; does not behave rudely, does not seek its own, is not provoked, thinks no evil; does not rejoice in iniquity, but rejoices in the truth; bears all things, believes all things, hopes all things, endures all things. Love never fails.[7]

Many of us would admit that our love for others does not mirror Paul's definition. If anything, we become impatient, self-seeking, and angry when our sources of love and security are often threatened. We must admit that human sources of love usually disappoint us. Our human love, from a sibling, friend, parent, pastor, spouse, or lover fails us as often as it delivers.

No human being loves us perfectly, but God does!

Love is laying down our life for another. We do not always have to physically die for them to show our love, but we may have to die to our own desires or agenda. Writing to the church at Ephesus, Paul reminds readers that they owe their salvation entirely to the undeserved grace of God. Grace refers to the unmerited love and joyful acceptance of God.

Grace is at once the objective, operative, and instrumental cause.[8]

Ephesians 2:8-9 (NKJV) For by grace you have been saved through faith, and that not of yourselves; it is the gift of God, not of works, lest anyone should boast.

Eighteenth century, theologian, cleric, and evangelist, John Wesley preached about three specific forms of God's grace: Prevenient grace, Justifying grace, and Sanctifying grace. These are not different kinds of grace - there is only one grace and that is God's divine unmerited love. However, as His love becomes more evident, our eyes are opened to receive God's love.

Both the Old Testament and the New use the metaphor of marriage to illustrate the relationship of humans with God. We can use that metaphor in describing Wesley's three forms of God's grace. Prevenient Grace is the love that God has for us - even while we are still sinners Jesus gave His life for us.[9] This can be likened to the courtship period, where the future bridegroom woos His bride. Justifying Grace can be equated to the marriage ceremony. Sanctifying grace then, is the continuing life as the couple grows together in love, affection, and begin to share one another's image. The Holy Spirit continues to sanctify us as we grow into the image of God.

A major factor in our failure to describe love is the limitation of the English language. In Greek, there are at least three different words which the Bible has translated as "love."

"Eros," describes a physical attraction such as a sexual relationship, or my craving for chocolate, mocha lattes. The English word "erotic" is derived from the Greek word "eros."

A familial or brotherly love is the Greek word "Phileo," which describes a relationship that develops between people sharing similar history, goals and purposes. The city of Philadelphia is the called the "City of Brotherly love." Phileo love grows between people who are moving toward the same goal. Picture a triangle with its base parallel to the ground. Put yourself at the left end of the base and a friend at the right end of the base. At the top point of the triangle, you can place an important goal. As you and your friend move closer to the goal, you also move closer to each other as the base line gets shorter. The love between us grows as we come closer to one another. Philos does not grow between persons who do not share a common commitment.

"He liked to walk alone, she liked to walk alone, they got married, and they walked alone together."

The absence of love is more often marked by indifference rather than conflict. Indifference results when people do not have the same commitments or interests. In the book of Revelation, the church at Philadelphia was favored by Jesus because they obeyed Jesus' commands, they had faith, hope and love for one another.

Phileo is distinguished from agape in that phileo more nearly represents tender affection. Jesus had a relationship with his father in heaven where He experienced natural affection.

*Mark 1:9-11 At that time Jesus came from Nazareth in Galilee and was baptized by John in the Jordan. As Jesus was coming up out of the water, he saw heaven being torn open and the Spirit descending on him like a dove. [11] And a voice came from heaven: "You are my Son, whom I love [**Phileo**]; with you I am well pleased."*

The most common word translated in the New Testament as "love" is the Greek word "Agape." Agape is the unconditional love that God has for all humanity. Agape usually describes God's loving transactions from a distance. But when the Bible describes God's love coming close to us and touching our hearts, the word often used is Phileo.

Pastor and author Jerry Cook writes[10]

"Agape love first exists, and then it affects the emotions. 'For God so loved the world that He sat in heaven and had warm feelings?' No, that's nonsense. 'For God so loved the world that He gave' (John 3:16). That's it! Agape is a volitional commitment to another that motivates us to act on his or her behalf. Every time we find a corresponding action to the concept of agape, it is a giving action.

Furthermore, agape involves the kind of giving that cannot be compensated. That concept of love is quite foreign to our culture. The mentality of this world leads us to love and give only when there is reason to assume that our love will be reciprocated. This reciprocity is tested carefully during a 'getting acquainted' time. If things look promising, and if our approach is met with acceptance and response, we risk a bit further, and a friendship is established. We first get acquainted and then move into love...sometimes."

In the kingdom of God, we first love and then move into acquaintance. Love is a commitment and operates independently of what we feel or do not feel.

Agape is a decision we make to love someone even when they are not lovable. Agape is a value-adding love. A newborn baby is a mess, it cries, messes its diapers, and cannot talk, yet the mother loves that child, and tends to its every need. That is how God loves us as we whine, make messes, and rebel.

Back to St Paul's love chapter, *"And now abide faith, hope, love, these three; but the greatest of these is love.*[11]*"* Love is greater than faith and hope. It is all about relationship and relationship is what we see in the Trinity, Father, Son, and Holy Spirit. As we become a part of that relationship, we can know the same love that the Father has for His Son[12].

We ask again, "What is love?" How do we define love? It is an impossible task to adequately define love.

God is love.[13] Since God is love, we must look to Him to define love. But that forces us into another dilemma: How do you define God? He is impossible to define. Therefore, it is not possible to fully define love, but we can grow in our love day by day.

> *If God is infinite, and if "God is love," then love is infinite, which means we will never reach the end of it. Even in the eternal life to come, we shall be forever increasing in love, forever plunging the infinite depths of God. Thus St. John describes love as the progress of eternity: Love has no boundary, and both in the present and in the future age we will never cease to progress in it, as we add light to light.[14]*

Early church monastic, St John of the Ladder (Climacus,) examines the means of ascending to the highest degree of religious perfection by a series of thirty steps. Each step recalls a year of the life of Christ. The most holy example of religious perfection is achieved at step number thirty.

> *The angels know how to discuss love, but even they are only able to do this according to their level of understanding. God is love, so the one who desires to describe this, attempts with dim eyes to weigh the sand in the sea. Love, from its very essence, is the likeness of God. As much as it possible for humans, in its action it is intoxication of the soul, and through its unique characteristic it is a spring of faith, and abyss of long-suffering, an ocean of lowliness. Love is fundamentally the exile of all opposing thoughts, for love thinks nothing evil.[15]*

If God is love, then our ability to love, reflects the God we worship and our understanding of that God.

> *The one who supposes it is possible to use mere words to explain the emotion and result of the love of the Lord precisely, blessed humbleness, elegantly, blessed innocence, sincerely, godly enlightenment, clearly, the fear of God, truly, steadfastness of the heart, honestly, and supposes that by his account of things of this type he will enlighten those who have not had the experience of them, is like a person who with words and analogies would like to give the concept of the sweetness of honey to others who have never tried it. Just as the latter speaks without effect, not to say babbles, so the first either gives the sense of having no experience of what he is relating, or he has become only a tool of vainglory.*[16]

While it may be impossible to define love, in the incarnation we have an example to emulate. God became a man in Jesus, the Christ. Jesus came that we might know God and if God is love, Jesus shows us what love is all about.

Chapter 5 - The Promise of the Father

And being assembled together with them, He commanded them not to depart from Jerusalem, but to wait for the Promise of the Father, "which," He said, "you have heard from Me; [Acts 1:4 (NKJV)]

We humans do not inherently have the capacity to love with all our heart, soul, mind, and strength. Our feeble attempts at loving God, ourselves, and others fail miserably no matter how hard we try under our own power. The only perfect love is from the God who is Love. In His infinite wisdom, He provided us a way in which we can, with His help, love properly. He has given to believers His Holy Spirit, God in us, providing us the power to live, love, and help others. It is only through this indwelling Spirit that we can genuinely love.

Jesus told His followers to stay in Jerusalem and He would send the "Promise of the Father," to empower them from on high.[17] The Holy Spirit was promised in the Old Testament through the prophets, Isaiah, Joel and Ezekiel.[18]

The promise of the Father is the Holy Spirit. The Holy Spirit is God's gift to believers to empower them to love and minister with creative and resurrection power.[19] The Holy Spirit is the third person in the triune Godhead, He is a person not a thing or it. Not a third God and not one third of God. The Holy Spirit is the very fullness of God Himself.

God is Spirit[20], and the Spirit of the holy God reflects the very nature of God. If we want to know what God is like, we can look at Jesus because Jesus is the visible manifestation of the invisible God.[21] If we want to know what the holy Spirit is like we also look at Jesus because the Holy Spirit is the reflection of the very nature of Jesus

Christ. Jesus said I am the truth and the light, and the Holy Spirit is the Spirit of Truth.[22]

We know that God is love, so the Holy Spirit is the spirit of love, perfectly revealed in Jesus Christ.

Theologian and author R. T. Kendall writes[23] about an English couple who became missionaries to Israel. Upon arrival at their home near Jerusalem, they noted a dove had come to live just outside their window. They felt this was a sign from God that He was with them as they were doing His work. After a few weeks, they realized that the dove would leave whenever a door would slam or there was any loud noise. They became concerned that the dove might fly away and never return. They figured that either the dove would have to adjust to their ways, or they would have to adjust to the ways of the dove's. They decided to adjust their lives to the dove's.

Watching the dove was a daily reminder to them that the heavenly Dove, the Holy Spirit, was there with them. It changed their lives forever.

When Jesus was baptized by John in the Jordan River, the Holy Trinity was revealed, Jesus arose from the water, The Father spoke from heaven, and the Holy Spirit descended like a dove, alighting on Jesus.

Kendall compares the characteristics of a dove to those of a pigeon. Doves never fight, while pigeons fight with each other all the time. Doves do not like noise, pigeons thrive on busy streets in cities. Doves are afraid of humans, pigeons are not. Doves are not territorial while pigeons defend their territory. Doves cannot be trained nor tamed while pigeons are often trained. Doves mate for life, while pigeons have many partners.

While the dove has long been a symbol of peace, God designated it as a symbol of the Holy Spirit. Jesus even describes a dove as harmless.[24] The fruit of the presence of the Spirit in a person's life is love, joy, peace, long-suffering, kindness, goodness, faithfulness, gentleness, and self-control.

The Holy Spirit is sensitive and can be grieved.[25] Grieving means to cause pain. It refers to our actions which hinder the Spirit from being Himself, from being what He could be in us. When He is not grieved in us, we will manifest His character, love, joy, peace, long-suffering, kindness, goodness, faithfulness, gentleness, self-control. Unforgiveness, anger, and bitterness grieve the Holy Spirit and make it almost impossible for us to love

The Holy Spirit can be quenched.[26] Jesus did no miracles in Nazareth because of the lack of faith which quenched the Holy Spirit. Quenching the Spirit refers to actions which hinder the Spirit from doing what He could do through us. When He is not quenched in us, we can manifest His power and love. Our lack of faith quenches our ability to love.

If we expect the Spirit to remain with us, it is essential that we do nothing to cause the dove to fly away. Kendall writes of the church.

"I suspect that this aspect of the sensitivity of the Holy Spirit's personality has resulted from the church's tendency to move on without Jesus, believing that He is still with us when he is not. We have taken Him for granted. It seems not to have crossed our minds that He has a dignity of His own and wants to be consulted, honored and recognized before we go on." [R. T. Kendall]

Earlier John the Baptist had proclaimed,

"I indeed baptize you with water unto repentance, but He who is coming after me is mightier than I, whose sandals I am not worthy to carry. He will baptize you with the Holy Spirit and fire." [Matthew 3:11 (NKJV)]

Then, just before Jesus ascended into heaven, He told His disciples,

"John baptized with water, but you shall be baptized in the Holy Spirit not many days from now.[27] "

The term "Baptized in the Holy Spirit" has come to mean different things to different people, but I like to think of it as meaning, to be immersed in the very nature of God, to be submerged in God's love, immersed in the dynamic, powerful, creating love of God, burying the old ways and being raised to new life in Jesus, completely saturating your whole being in the Spirit of God, and be filled with the fullness of God.[28]

Baptism in the Holy Spirit is being immersed in God's love until we have died to self and raised to a new life in Jesus Christ

The average Christian, although truly professing Christ, operates largely on his own power, making his own decisions, living on his own strength, controlling his own life, and attempting to love others with his own strength.

I could never tell Jesus how much I loved Him until the Holy Spirit dwelling in me, guided me. It takes the Holy Spirit to reveal to us the full love, wonder, and glory of Jesus Christ.

For Jesus Himself said, *"He (the Holy Spirit) will glorify Me, for He will take what is Mine and declare it to you."[John16:14]*

The Fruit of the Holy Spirit is the presence of the nature of God in the life of the believer. It is the Spirit being Himself in us. God produces this Fruit. Whereas spiritual gifts are essential to the work of the Church and the Kingdom of God, spiritual fruit prepares us to live in the Kingdom of God now and through eternity.

Love never fails. but whether there are prophecies, they will fail; whether there are tongues, they will cease; whether there is knowledge, it will vanish away." (1 Corinthians 13:8)

Chapter 6 - The Father's Love

For God so loved the world that He gave His only begotten Son, that
whoever believes in Him should not perish but have everlasting life.
[John 3:16 (NKJV)]

We need the love of God. If we want to love others, we need God's love to first shine on us. Loving others well flows freely from those whose hearts have received God's love. His Love is patient, kind, neither boastful nor proud, not self-seeking, or readily angered, keeping no record of wrongs. Love protects and hopes for the best in our hearts. God perseveres on our behalf and helps us receive Himself as the Source of love that never fails.

Our ability to love is rooted in finding and securing a real, unfailing love. The only way we can be secure in love is being loved by a source of love that is strong enough to break through the defenses, we have created, and enter deep into our heart.

If we want to be free to love fully, we need love to first shine on us. Loving others properly can only flow freely from those whose hearts are receiving an abundance of unfailing love, which comes only from God.

Jesus Christ is the quintessential model of how we are to love. Even many non-Christians, who do not believe He is God or Savior, freely admit that his life reflects a demonstration of true unfailing love. His teachings and earthly life provide a road map guiding us to that idyllic world where love reigns.

Too often, our failure to love results from not being able to trust. We may want to love them, but deep down in our soul we are afraid that they do not have our best interests at heart, and if we love them, becoming vulnerable, we can be hurt badly. It is equally true that that same fear keeps us from receiving love from someone we do not trust.

From even a cursory reading of the New Testament, especially the four Gospels, it is not hard for most to realize that Jesus does in fact love us and has our best interests at heart. Children of Christian parents have grown up hearing the words of the song, "Jesus Loves Me."

While Jesus' love is not universally accepted throughout the world, it is much easier to accept the fact of His love for us than to believe that God, the Father, loves me. There are many that see God as a demanding and angry master ready to punish wrong doers. This is a result of misreading the Old Testament and a transference of personal father issues to the Heavenly Father.

God the Father loves us with the same love and intensity that He loves His Son Jesus. Jesus died on the cross and rose from the dead to secure us in that love. His act of love on the cross reveals the unchanging truth that God loves us. The cross reveals to us that God's love is more powerful than any other love we have experienced. The cross proclaims to us that nothing can separate us from God's love

> *1 John 4:10 (NKJV) In this is love, not that we loved God, but that He loved us and sent His Son to be the propitiation for our sins.*

Jesus had a relationship with his Father in heaven where He experienced love. Then, when it was time for Him to begin His ministry, He went down from Nazareth to Galilee to be baptized by John in the Jordan River. When Jesus came up out of the water, heaven was torn open, the Holy Spirit descended upon Him like a dove, and His Father spoke to Him from Heaven.[29]

> *"You are my Son, whom I love; with you I am well pleased."*

The Father gave Jesus the reassurance that His human heart required.

When said from the heart the three most powerful words in the English language are, "I Love You!"

If we hear them from our earthly father when we are young, they have a powerful effect for good. If we do not hear them when we are young, insecurities result which can undermine our success in life. Jesus heard those words, and his heart was secure.

"Yes! I am my father's son. He loves me."

Satan tried to derail Jesus from His mission, by tempting Him to prove His Sonship by turning stones into bread. Jesus did not bite; He remembered and trusted every word that His father had spoken. He did not have to prove His identity. He did not have to prove His value. He did not have to prove that He was loved.

Many of us feel a need to test whether we are loved. The enemy of our soul tempts us to prove our self-worth. We need to avoid temptation by being secure in the fact that God loves us.

As we face all the challenges of life, we need to be secure in the love of God and hear Him say to us,

"You are my child, I love you."

Jesus heard that same reassuring voice on the Mount of Transfiguration and in the Garden of Gethsemane, and He wants us to know the Father Heart of God that He has revealed. He wants to win us over to His sweet and powerful love.

On His last night with His disciples, Jesus told them He would soon be gone and that they would have to carry on without Him. They knew how strong was the relationship that Jesus had with His Father but were not sure of their own relationship with God. That may be like the place in which many of us find ourselves. What are we to do?

Jesus told them how they could follow in His footsteps:

In that day you will ask in my name. I am not saying that I will ask the Father on your behalf. No, the Father himself loves you because you have loved me and have believed that I came from God. [John 16:26-27]

You and I have direct access to the Father when we come in Jesus' name. Even more astounding is that when we love Jesus, we receive the love of His father.

The Greek word translated here as "love" in verse 27 is the more familiar form "phileo," not "agape." Agape describes God's loving transactions from a distance. But when the Bible describes God's love coming close to us and touching our hearts, the word more often used is "phileo." Phileo is distinguished from agape in that phileo more nearly represents tender affection. This means that the Father not only loves you because He created you, but He really likes you with a natural affection. This natural affection is available to all who love Jesus.

Once we really know the Father's love, we can break free of the need to prove ourselves and can freely love without the fear of being rejected or hurt.

The late theologian J. I. Packer writes[30]

> *You sum up the whole of New Testament religion if you describe it as the knowledge of God as one's Holy Father. If you want to judge how well a person understands Christianity, find out how much he makes of the thought of being God's child, and having God as His Father. If this is not the thought that prompts and controls his worship and prayers and his whole outlook on life, it means he does not understand Christianity very well at all. For everything that Christ taught, everything that makes the New Testament new...is summed up in the knowledge of the Fatherhood of God. Father is the Christian name for God.*

The problem in understanding Who God is, becomes mired in the semantics of the word "Father." Today in the United States, forty percent of children sleep in a home in which their father does not live. Before they are eighteen, a staggering fifty percent of the children will spend a significant amount of time living separate from their father. Some fathers have abandoned the family physically through divorce, separation, or job location. Even when there is not physical separation, there is often an emotional separation resulting in poor relationships with fathers due to work schedules, alcoholism, drug abuse, and fathers absorbed in their own problems.

This situation has been increasing since the end of World War II. Many of us grew up in families where our fathers were too busy for us. Many Children were rejected, ignored, or never able to live up to the expectations of their fathers.

> *The deepest search in life, it seemed to me, the thing that in one way or another was central to all living was man's search to find a father, not merely the father of his flesh, not merely the lost father of his youth, but the image of strength and wisdom external to his need and superior to his hunger, to which belief and power of his own life could be united.*[31]

Up until the time I was ten, I hardly saw my father. He was an alcoholic and even when he was not drinking, he was working odd hours. While he was an extremely outgoing and friendly man, we had very little close contact. In those early years, I never knew the love of a father. I am sure he loved me, but that love was not manifested and there was nothing tangible on which to hang. As a result, in my mind, my Heavenly Father was distant and too busy to care about me.

Attributing to God, the attitudes and characteristics of our earthly father is a common tendency. If your earthly father was harsh and demanding, that is the way you might see God the Father. If your earthly father was absent or distant, that's the way you might see God the Father.

We all grow up seeking the warmth of affectionate love. We look first to our parents, especially our fathers. If we receive the love we are looking for, then our tanks are filled. If not, we go through life trying to find this love in other relationships. However, the original father's emptiness remains. Ultimately, there is nothing in the world that can take the place of a father's love. Our pursuit of this love is often futile and leaves us empty. When we accept Jesus as our Lord and Savior, we must remind ourselves that Jesus wants to introduce us to His Father.

I am convinced that we will not be secure in love until we receive God's love for us as our Father. Still, many of us struggle with God as Father, because our human images of "father love" have often been inadequate and distorted.

Jesus taught us about the Father's love in the parable of the two sons. A man had two sons. One day the younger son came to his father and told him he wanted all his inheritance now as he wanted to leave the family and make his own life. The father gave him what he had asked for and allowed him to leave. The young son blew his inheritance far off in a strange land, and ended up destitute, feeding hogs to survive. He realized what a mess he had made of his life and decided to go home and see if his father would take him on as a servant. His father's servants lived much better than he was living.

> *Luke 15:20-24 (NKJV) And he arose and came to his father. But when he was still a great way off, his father saw him and had compassion, and ran and fell on his neck and kissed him. And the son said to him, 'Father, I have sinned against heaven and in your sight, and am no longer worthy to be called your son.' But the father said to his servants, 'Bring out the best robe and put it on him and put a ring on his hand and sandals on his feet. And bring the fatted calf here and kill it, and let us eat and be merry; for this my son was dead and is alive again; he was lost and is found.' And they began to be merry.*

Our heavenly Father is a watching and waiting, running, weeping, laughing, embracing, and kissing God. My Heavenly Father is so much more affectionate than my earthly Father.

The word "Prodigal," means extravagant, squandering, wasteful, reckless, and lavish. That was the son wasting his life on high living. When he returns, his father throws a robe over him, puts a ring on his finger, puts sandals on his feet, and throws a party for him. The father's love is prodigal. His love is extravagant, squandering, wasteful, reckless, and lavish. Jesus told this parable to describe the love that God, the Father, has for us.

The older son does not come to the party, in fact, he is still outside when the parable closes. One of the most amazing moments in the story occurs when the father leaves the party and goes out to the older brother to invite him to come to the party at the father's house. The older brother is angry and upset, he sees the prodigality of the Father's love for his brother and gets angry. After all, he had been working hard all these years to earn the Father's love and did not like it when kid brother comes home and is invited to the father's table. Just like the pharisees who saw the tax collectors and sinners hanging around Jesus, he had been striving hard to earn the father's love, yet the father loved both sons with his prodigal love.

In His priestly prayer,[32] Jesus reveals a truth which is hard for us to apprehend, *God the Father loves us with the same love that He has for Jesus.*

In this portion of His prayer, Jesus makes four statements:

"I have made you known to them." Jesus revealed the Father. He made known the infinite splendor, awesome beauty, and eternal loveliness of His Father. Every aspect of His ministry reflects the indescribable loveliness of God the Father. He taught us to call God, "Abba." The ministry of Jesus was most significantly defined by His reflection of the infinite glory and splendor of the Father. When people heard Jesus' words, observed His lifestyle, and beheld His perfectly

balanced personality and flawless character, they received a glimpse of what God the Father is like. It was Christ's honor and glory to reveal the Father. Yet you and I have the same glory.

....and will continue to make You known. He will continue to reveal the Father through the ministry of the Holy Spirit. Christ's greatest passion is to continue to make known the Father.

"In order that the love you have for me may be in them." The purpose of Jesus making the Father known is so that the love of the Father might be in us. Jesus is praying that the body of Christ will love Him, in the same way that the father loves Him. The Father desires a people who are awakened in their affections and passions for Jesus. God wants a passionate church that loves Jesus as the Father loves Him.

"and that I myself may be in them." First Jesus says, I have made You known to them. Then He says He will continue to make the Father known.

Why? So that the same love the Father has for Jesus would fill and energize the hearts of those who believe Him.

Then he says, *"I will be in them."* The quality of love the Father has for the Son will dwell in his people, manifesting His overflowing life through them.

Chapter 7 - Love God

And you shall love the Lord your God with all your heart, with all your soul, with all your mind, and with all your strength. [Mark 12:30 (NKJV)]

Love requires space in our hearts for the things we love. It requires actions that demonstrate that we love. Space and actions may be limited in our lives. We often hear people say they have no room in their lives to add a new friend or no time available to show their love for others.

Loving God requires a place in your heart and loving activities. It is a matter of priorities where you spend your time and love. Most of us will spend our love on things that provide immediate gratification. We often waste it on people or things that are not healthy for us.

In our busy world, there are many people who do not have the time or the inclination to spend their time or love on God. They have other priorities, family, friends, career, money, or status. They take God for granted; that He will always be there and when they get through their current crisis, then they will seek the Lord.

Ancient Israel had many similarities with today's world. In the eighth century before Christ, the prophet Hosea presented the word of God to Israel. It was a time in that nation's history not unlike our nation today and other nations around the world.

Israel was enjoying the best of times under King Jeroboam II. They had been experiencing unparalleled prosperity; and yet they had sunk to the lowest moral depths of their two-hundred-year history. They had entered adulterous relationships with the gods of the Canaanites that lived around them.

As a result, God was about to use their enemies as an instrument of His judgment.

Hosea was called by God to declare impending judgment on the Northern Kingdom. He called Hosea to experience things in his own personal life that would equip him to understand how God felt about

Israel. Hosea married a woman who became an adulteress. She left Him and sought-after other men.

Through the prophet, God made three charges against Israel.

Hear the word of the LORD, You children of Israel, For the LORD brings a charge against the inhabitants of the land: "There is no emeth, or chesed, or Da-ath Elohim in the land.[Hosea 4:1 (NKJV)]

Israel lacked three essential qualities required by God: Emeth, Chesed, and Da-ath Elohim.

The first charge is there is no "emeth." This Hebrew word is often translated as "truth" or "faithfulness." God states there is no dependability, consistency, or commitment in the nation. This word carries an underlying sense of certainty or dependability. God wants consistent dependability in His people. He desires trustworthiness in those who choose to follow Him. It is not enough for followers of God to follow Him only when it is convenient. In Israel, there was no personal commitment by the people. They made treaties with foreign countries, then broke the treaties when it was no longer convenient. Marriage vows meant nothing, adultery was at an all-time high, divorce was rampant. Israel had made a commitment to God to obey the Law. But they ran after the god's of the Canaanites.

We live in a day when truth, commitment, consistency, and dependability are out of style. There is no such thing as truth in Post Modernism. We jump from job to job and from relationship to relationship. It's all about me and my comfort. It's a disposable age. - throw it away and get a new one. This is true with the latest tech gadget, home appliances, and even human relationships. There is no commitment to family. No commitment to friends. No commitment to God.

God's second charge is "there is no chesed in Israel." This word is often translated as "mercy," A better translation would be "steadfast love." Chesed is the type of love that the Moabite woman, Ruth, had for her mother-in-law Naomi in the book of Ruth. It is the kind of love that God has shown for His people Israel. Steadfast love requires actions. Israel did not return God's steadfast love. She was not loyal to His commandments.

Steadfast love is missing in our world right now. We love conditionally.

"I will love you as long as you make me feel good. I will love God as long as He gives me what I want."

If you face hardship, will you still love God as did Job?

God lays a third indictment against Israel, "There is no Knowledge of God." (Da ath Elohim.) This term is the same term used to describe an intimate relationship. Adam "Da-athed" Eve and they conceived a child. God is saying that the people have no intense, intimate, emotional relationship with God. This does not mean there is no awareness of God - people may know about God, but There is no inner attachment to God.

What God wants is an inner dedication, not just routine ceremonies. The loss of da-ath Elohim is the real undoing of Israel, and it is the undoing of much of the church throughout the world today.

God disciplined the rebellious nation, but His love remained steadfast and He provided reconciliation and restoration.

"I will heal their backsliding, I will love them freely, For My anger has turned away from him. I will be like the dew to Israel; He shall grow like the lily and lengthen his roots like Lebanon. His branches shall spread; His beauty shall be like an olive tree, and his fragrance like Lebanon. Those who dwell under his shadow shall return; They shall be revived like grain, and grow like a vine. Their scent shall be like the wine of Lebanon.[Hosea 14:4-7 (NKJV)]

Even when we turn our back on God, His love will never fail. That is how we should return that love to Him.

Jesus spent His time in service to others. So, if you are looking for an icon of love, you cannot do better than to love and become like Jesus. If you want to become a lover of people, a good first step is to love Jesus. The more we come to love Jesus, the more we will become like Him. The more we become like Jesus, the more we will love ourselves and others.

The church will never love one another until it first loves God. Some will put almost any good thing ahead of loving God. We often make Bible study, doctrinal purity, evangelism, and other good things more important than loving God.

How can we mere mortals love the omnipotent, omniscient, omnipresent creator of the universe? How can we show our love for anyone?

Jesus showed His love for His Father, by being obedient to the Father's wishes, so much so that He laid down His life for us.

By this we know love, because He laid down His life for us. And we also ought to lay down our lives for the brethren.[1 John 3:16]

Following His example, in obedience to God, we also ought to lay down our lives for those we love. Most of us will not become true martyrs, literally dying to save them, but we should lay down our agenda and our selfish desires for those we love. We love Jesus by obeying His call on our lives. It is no longer our desires that we seek after, but His. We must lay down our plans and what we would desire in favor of God's plan. Interestingly, it has been my experience that whenever I have canceled my agenda and followed the Lord's call, I was not only happier, but more successful in what I was doing.

Jesus, on the night He was betrayed by Judas, went to the Garden of Gethsemane to pray. His prayer is our prayer, *"Nevertheless not my will but your's be done. [Luke 22:42 (NKJV)]"*

Jesus told us how to show our love for Him. *"If you love Me, keep My commandments* [John 14:15 (NKJV)]."

Our first step in loving God is to obey His commandments.

Step two in loving God is to love one another

> *"A new commandment I give to you, that you love one another; as I have loved you, that you also love one another. By this all will know that you are My disciples, if you have love for one another." [John 13:34-35]*

Writing to the churches he oversaw, the Apostle John further explained what it meant to love one another:

> *.....we should love one another, not as Cain, who was of the wicked one and murdered his brother. He who does not love his brother abides in death....... Whoever hates his brother is a murderer, and you know that no murderer has eternal life abiding in him. By this we know love, because He laid down His life for us. And we also ought to lay down our lives for the brethren. But whoever has this world's goods, and sees his brother in need, and shuts up his heart from him, how does the love of God abide in him? .... Let us not love in word or in tongue, but in deed and in truth. [1 John 3:11-24]*

In the Gospel of Matthew, Jesus described additional actions deemed important if we are to love Him and love one another.

> *"Then the King will say to those on His right hand, 'Come, you blessed of My Father, inherit the kingdom prepared for you from the foundation of the world: for I was hungry and*

you gave Me food; I was thirsty, and you gave Me drink; I was a stranger, and you took Me in; I was naked, and you clothed Me; I was sick, and you visited Me; I was in prison, and you came to Me.' Then the righteous will answer Him, saying, 'Lord, when did we see You hungry and feed You, or thirsty and give You drink? When did we see You a stranger and take You in, or naked and clothe You? Or when did we see You sick, or in prison, and come to You?' And the King will answer and say to them, 'Assuredly, I say to you, inasmuch as you did it to one of the least of these My brethren, you did it to Me.'"[Matthew 25:34-40 (NKJV)]

Loving God requires humility.

Obedience is surely part of loving God, but it is not all that is required. Conformity to His word can lead to pride. Humility is the antidote for pride.

Jesus humbled Himself when He became obedient to the Father. Only Jesus could experience coming down from the throne of heaven and becoming a man. When God sits enthroned in heaven's glory, there is no one He obeys. Jesus had to leave this glory and become in appearance as a man to become obedient. The point of Jesus' obedience on earth was the endurance of suffering. Again, this is something He could only learn by experience after the incarnation.

As it is written: though He was a Son, yet He learned obedience by the things which He suffered.[33]

The extent of Jesus' obedience is shown by the fact that he went to the point of death, even the death of the cross. Crucifixion was such a shameful death that it was not permitted for Roman citizens. Any victim of crucifixion was considered by the Jews to be particularly cursed by God. Death on the cross was the opposite from the throne of God. Jesus came all the way down to the most despised death of all, a condemned criminal on the accursed cross. Even the death on the cross shows that there is no limit to what God will do to demonstrate His love and saving power.

Psalm 119 is the longest chapter of the entire Bible, and it is a testimony to the blessings of obedience to God. The theme continues throughout Blessed are those who walk in the law of the Lord, who seek Him with the whole heart, walk in His ways, keep His precepts diligently, and keep His statutes.

Loving God is not only obedience, but it is also feeling. Obedience without a fervor for God is not love but discipline. And if discipline is all we have; in the end it will fail us. In his paraphrase of the Bible, "The Message," Eugene Peterson translates Mark 12:30; *so love the Lord God with all your passion and prayer and intelligence and energy.*

How do we love God with passion or intense feeling? We must understand two important truths. First, we must know Who God is, and then we must know who we are in relation to God. For this we may need to renew our vision of God.

Suppose you were awakened in the middle of the night with a knock on your door. You get out of bed, go to the door, and ask, "Who is it?"

From outside you hear a deep resonant voice reply, "It is Me, God, I want to talk to you."

What do you think He wants to talk to you about?

When you open the door, what kind of expression does He have on His face?

In your most private thoughts, how do you envision God?

What is He like?

Your entire spiritual future is related to how you answer these questions in the secret place of your heart. If you have an inaccurate picture of God, it will have a negative impact on you. We must understand, Who God is, what He has done, what we can receive, and what we must do. The church has placed most of its emphasis on the last three; forgiveness of sins, our inheritance, and how we should live, but less on the character and personality of the Trinity.

We are awakened with overwhelming feelings of love when the awesome God, who is love, is fully revealed to us. It takes the power of God to make God known. It takes the knowledge of God to enable mankind to love God, and it takes God to love God.

It takes God to know God. The Holy Spirit teaches us about God. The Holy Spirit in us will use the release of knowledge to awaken a sense of deep urgency for intimacy with God. The source of our fervent affection for Jesus will not be in us naturally, it only comes as the Holy Spirit reveals in us God's glory and His work on the cross. Our love for Christ comes from encountering just a brief, dim glimpse of who God is, and what He has done.

A church filled with the knowledge of God, reflecting His glory, and consumed with a passion for Jesus will be prepared to engage in the great conflicts to come.

Chapter 8 - Love Yourself

Then God saw everything that He had made, and indeed it was very good. [Genesis 1:31 (NKJV)]

After God created the heavens and earth, He said it was good. After He created the Sun, moon, plants, birds, and animals, He said it was good.

But after He created man and woman, he said everything He created was VERY GOOD. That includes you and me, we were created in this image of God and He says we are VERY GOOD.

Still many of us disagree with God and do not like ourselves, let alone really love ourselves. But God does not make junk.

King David who failed as many times as he succeeded in following God, could still praise God, and say, *"I am fearfully and wondrously made." (Psalm 139:14)*

He acknowledges that his Creator did a great work in creating. In acknowledging how marvelous are God's creation, he also infers that he himself is wonderful. In this the Psalmist acknowledges both his love for his Creator and his love for himself. Unfortunately, few of us can say, with the same assurance, that we love ourselves.

Anyone who does not love himself cannot genuinely love another.

Let us do a little imagining. Suppose you are sitting in heaven and Jesus comes up to you and says, "I want you to go to earth for me."

Would you want to go?

Would you want to go to the same time and place in which you were born?

Would you want to be born the same sex that you were born?

Would you want the same physical appearance?

Would you want the same parents?

If you would change any of the above, you have a false image of who God created you to be and you may be in rebellion against God.

We do not see ourselves very clearly. The search for our true self often results in little more than a few clues that only define a part of who we are. Our true image is distorted. It is as if we are in a carnival house of mirrors that reflect a distorted image of ourselves. Some mirrors show us as fatter, skinnier, taller, or shorter. These are not our true shape. They are merely distortions of the mirror that make us appear different.

The people in our life are like those mirrors, reflecting a distorted image. This leads us to believe we are what they see, and that image becomes our self-image. Extremely critical parents provide an impression of inadequacy, ex-spouses may provide another view, our boss or colleagues provide their view, and friends and associates have other views. These images, reflected back to us from other human beings, are flawed. They provide only a tiny piece of our image.

Our self-image is <u>not</u> based upon all these little pieces. It is <u>not</u> based upon what others think about us. Instead, our self-image is based upon what we think others think about us, which may not be what they really think.

Even more important to our self-image is, what we think the most important person in our life, thinks about us. That is why parents, spouses, friends, and employers can have such an impact on one's self-image. Children first look to parents for love, acceptance, and encouragement. Later in life, a spouse or employer becomes that most significant person who establishes one's view of self.

There are many issues which negatively affect our love for self:

- Life experience; parental neglect, a tyrannical teacher or boss, and peer acceptance.
- Physical, sexual, or emotional abuse.
- Real or imagined physical defects.
- Lack of a healthy parent relationship

All these factors can add up to a lowering of self-love or self-esteem. Trauma may also affect our self-image as it can bring up the question of why did this happen to me, or why God did not prevent my suffering?

Then there is self-blame, "What did I do to deserve this?"

Research has shown that low self-esteem manifests itself with heavy self-criticism; dissatisfaction with life; hypersensitivity to criticism; resentment against critics; feelings of being attacked (paranoia); chronic indecision; and an exaggerated fear of making mistakes.

Lack of self-love can result in an excessive desire to please; perfectionism leading to frustration when perfection is not achieved; neurotic guilt, exaggerating the magnitude of past mistakes; hostility, general defensiveness, and irritability without any proximate cause; pessimism and a general negative outlook; envy; or a general resentment.

With low self-esteem, one sees temporary setbacks as permanent, intolerable conditions. They tend to be critical of themselves. Some depend on the approval and praise of others when evaluating their own self-worth. Others may measure their likability in terms of successes or accept themselves if they succeed but will not if they fail.

Dr. Ken Tittle was a medical doctor who forfeited a lucrative medical practice in the North Eastern US to aid immigrant farm workers in California. Later, after settling down in the border town of Calexico, across from Mexicali, Mexico, Ken noted a huge number of post-polio victims in Mexicali. When the polio vaccine had first been sent there, a problem developed with storage practices resulting in a vast number of healthy children who were given the disease by an injection of what everyone thought would protect them. Seeing such a great need, Dr Tittle founded Mariposa (Butterfly in Spanish) Ministries to aid the damaged, broken, and misshapen victims of that dreaded disease.

While speaking at a conference on prayer and healing in the mountains of Southern California, Ken pointed to the panoramic landscape outside the retreat center, and exclaimed, "How marvelous are God's works."

He then offered these words of comfort to the entire group, "Yet every tree, every branch, every leaf of that beautiful vista, is damaged, broken, or misshapen."

We are all damaged, broken, and misshapen in some way, yet all together and individually we reflect the glory of God, Who created us in His own image.

Andrew Comiskey[34] tells the story of a beautiful painting by a famous artist:

Suppose a famous painter created a beautiful portrait in his distinctive style. It was unbelievably valuable and hung in a museum where everyone could see it and marvel at its beauty. But then it was stolen. Since it was so distinctive and the product of that great artist, it could not be sold without the authorities catching the thieves. The painting was mistreated and hidden away for many years in an attic where it gathered dust and acquired further damage. It became only a dim reflection of its earlier glory and beauty.

The artist searches and searches for his lost painting until it is finally found, but it is in terrible condition. The dirt and grime hide its true form and the brightly vibrant original colors. But the master painter finally has his property back. Gently and with unerring accuracy and skill the master artist restores his work, removing layers of filth and repairing the damage, enabling his true creation to emerge.

Jesus is the master painter, and we are the painting. He loves us so much that He wants to reclaim that true image in each of us.

The only way to get an accurate picture of who you are is from Jesus. He created you in His image. In His great love for you, He wants to restore you to the true being which He created. He alone can call forth that true self. And as we respond to His initiative in our lives, our true personhood comes forth. His love awakens us and calls us out of the shadows of our lesser selves. Through His reflection, we become who we truly are. Jesus alone possesses the knowledge of that true self; we see ourselves only in part.

After God created the heavens and the earth and all the plants and animals, it was time for His greatest creation.

> *"Let Us make man in Our image, according to Our likeness; let them have dominion over the fish of the sea, over the birds of the air, and over the cattle, over all the earth and over every creeping thing that creeps on the earth." So God created man in His own image; in the image of God He created him; male and female He created them. [Genesis 1:26-27 (NKJV)]*

Humanity alone bears God's image. That means we are called to represent and somehow reveal God on this earth. We are like little mirrors intended to reflect the glory of God. Bearing that image is the most profound and authentic part of our humanity. Our image shines forth as we welcome Jesus into our lives. It is only through responding to Jesus and His initiative in our lives that we can discover who and what we truly are.

> *"Your real, new self (which is Christ's and also yours, and yours just because it is His) will not come as long as you are looking for it. It will come when you are looking for Him." [C. S. Lewis]*

As we seek to know Jesus better, more of our true self is reclaimed. It is then that we come to understand the higher and truer purpose of our humanity. Our role is to love God and other human beings. God created us to know Him, to have fellowship with Him and to worship Him.

Our emergence into the true self must be worked out in the real hard ground of life. And that is where we need help. That is where we need other followers of Jesus to help remind us of who we truly are. The truth is we are still so defined by our own broken perceptions that we need encouraging words from Him, who we are becoming like. The word comes from God, but He uses people to bless us and remind us of the truth of our worth and high calling as bearers of His image.

The one thing that can fill the emptiness inside us is knowing and experiencing the Love of God. If our self-image is based upon what we think the most important person in our life thinks of us, then we must make sure that God is that most important person. Then we must believe how very much He loves us.

Our lives will be transformed as we understand and experience the love of God. When we can receive God's love deep down in our hearts, it will change our lives.

We will then have our identity as children of the Creator, the living God. We will realize our extreme value, established by the cost paid for our salvation, the Father's only begotten Son.

We will have confidence because we do not have to prove our value.

We will be able to take risks because failure does not mean we are bad.

We will understand why we were created and placed in our unique circumstances.

We know that God has a vocation planned for our lives.

If the most important person in your life is Jesus, and you know He loves you, you will be able to love yourself.

At times we can be harsher critics of ourselves than is God. While God forgives us our sins when we confess them[35], we often will not forgive ourselves. It is as if we have higher standards than does God.

Before we are able to genuinely love others, we must deal with our own issues of self-worth and the fear of rejection.

Chapter 9 – Enemies of Love

See to it that no one misses the grace of God and that no bitter root grows up to cause trouble and defile many.

Hebrews 12:15 (NIV)

Deep within many hearts, lay hidden issues that prevent on from freely loving others. These issues will also deter others from loving us properly. Unwarranted fear, anger, bitterness, and judgmentalism all have a hidden root cause which is often unforgiveness.

Anyone who would otherwise want to love us, might refuse to scale the obstacles which we put in their path. Most find it too hard to love and will not invest the time and energy required to care for us on the slim chance that a satisfying relationship might develop.

If we want to love and be loved, it is up to us to deal with our personal issues and make it easier for someone to care enough to grow in a relationship with us.

Fear of failure and fear of rejection cause many to give up not only on love, but to give up on any worthy activity.

"There is no fear in love; but perfect love casts out fear, because fear involves torment. But he who fears has not been made perfect in love." [1 John 4:18 (NKJV)]

The perfection of love is confidence, Lack of fear! Love and fear cannot co-exist. If we are fearful, it is not a problem with God's love. The problem is in our ability to receive His Love.

So many of us have been broken in our own wholeness to the degree that we cannot receive His love fully.

We do not have to be afraid of someone who loves us. God who loves us also wants the best for us. Therefore, we can trust Him, if we trust Him, we do not fear Him.

Fear can be positive. It can protect you, such as fear of sticking your hand in a boiling pot, fear of crossing a busy street, and fear of disobeying God. It is the difference between fearing something to keep you from doing something stupid and fearing things over which you have no control.

The issue is control, who is in charge. We fear not being in control.

"For God has not given us a spirit of fear, but of power and of love and of a sound mind." [2 Timothy 1:7 (NKJV)]

The root cause of fear is embedded deep within the soul and may need ministry to remove it. The Spirit's work of adoption in our lives is the opposite of the work of the spirit of fear which leads to slavery. Deep fears of failing and of rejection are the greatest obstacles to experiencing love.

Throughout my life I was unable to break free of trying to work for love and acceptance. I was afraid of rejection, so I worked harder to earn acceptance. I was paralyzed with fear in asking girls for dates and feared meeting new people.

When first facing someone new, my chest would tighten up and my mind would turn to Jello. Being so overwhelmed by panic, I would freeze. It was a fear that they would reject me.

I was also afraid of failure, so only tackled things when I knew I could succeed. In school, I never let anyone put my name up to run for an office, because failure meant rejection.

I have always loved to write, but for many years, I did not submit anything for publishing in fear of the pain of rejection.

When employers and others realized I could write, they often paid me to go write something. When they commissioned me to write, there would be no rejection letter.

Then one day I heard God's voice, *"You are my son, I love you and you can never fail in my sight."*

Within a month of hearing the Fathers voice Rita and I left the security of ministry in a denominational church, to follow His call into a new region of the country and a totally new ministry.

Defeating the enemies of love requires dealing with the root causes of our insecurities, anger, and bitterness. The first step is to identify those roots.

When God created the world, he set up absolute unchangeable laws. These laws are for our benefit and they are to be obeyed or we accept the consequences. There are physical laws and spiritual laws.

The law of gravity is one of the physical laws. If I drop a plate from the table, it will fall to the floor. It falls whether or not I believe in gravity. If the dish breaks when it hits the floor, it does not mean that God is angry at the dish. It just broke because I let it go and gravity took over.

Isaac Newton's third law of motion is that for every action there is an equal and opposite reaction. If I throw a ball at the wall it will bounce back to me, (unless it first hits a lady in the second row. This happened one evening as I was demonstrating this law – broke her glasses.)

In chemistry we learned that a formula must be balanced on both sides of the equals (=) sign. If there is an imbalance, cataclysmic things can happen, like explosions or if you have ever been up in the air on a teeter-totter when the person on the other side got off, you can realize what might happen.

We are obedient to God's physical laws and as we progress in understanding of them, we can make airplanes that fly, land men on the moon, and send spacecraft to Mars.

Just as God set physical laws in place, He also set in place spiritual laws. We cannot violate God's physical laws without consequences, and at the same time, we think we can disregard God's spiritual laws without facing their consequences.

As is in the case of the physical laws, if we disobey spiritual laws, there are consequences. Violation of God's spiritual laws do have consequences.

Let's look at a few spiritual laws:

Honor your mother and father:

> *Honor your father and your mother, as the LORD your God has commanded you, that your days may be long, and that it may be well with you in the land which the LORD your God is giving you.* Deuteronomy 5:16 (NKJV)

The spiritual, law expressed here tells us that life will go well for us in every area in which you can honor your parents. The corollary of that law is life will not go well for us in every area in which we cannot honor them. God loves us but also knows that when we break this law we can be hurt.

Judge not lest you be judged.

> *"Judge not, that you be not judged. For with what judgment you judge, you will be judged; and with the measure you use, it will be measured back to you."*

[Matthew 7:1-2]

Therefore you are inexcusable, O man, whoever you are who judge, for in whatever you judge another you condemn yourself; for you who judge practice the same things. [Romans 2:1 (NKJV)]

We will suffer in our lives in the same areas in which we have judged others. Those things that offend us about others are usually the very things with which we have problems.

Whenever we judge someone, we set in motion a law, the result of which is; we will do to others those things for which we condemn them.

The Law of sowing and reaping

Do not be deceived, God is not mocked; for whatever a man sows, that he will also reap. [Galatians 6:7 (NKJV)]

This is like the law of balance. if we sow love, we will reap blessing. If we sow hatred, we reap destruction. As children we may sin and not know it, but we may reap it later as adults.

A corollary of sowing and reaping is the law of multiplication. As we sow, we will reap but it will increase. The first command that God gave to Adam and Eve to be fruitful and multiply. Jesus was angry at the person who buried his talents, and we are told to lay up treasures in heaven not on earth.

God made the law of increase and sowing and reaping so we could sow good deeds and receive blessings. That was before sin entered the world. When sin entered the same laws of sowing and reaping, and multiplication applied but if we so evil we reap destruction.

Forgiveness is not Optional

"For if you forgive men their trespasses, your heavenly Father will also forgive you. But if you do not forgive men their trespasses, neither will your Father forgive your trespasses.
[Matthew 6:14-15 (NKJV)]

Christians cannot afford the luxury of even one small grudge. A grudge is like sand thrown in a well-oiled machine. It steals our health, our joy, and our relationship with God and with others. If God has not forgiven us, then we do not have a relationship with him.

It is not easy to really forgive in our heart. We may say a quick, *"I forgive you,"* but it may not reach our heart. True forgiveness is in the heart. It is not just saying the words. Our heart knows better we're still bitter and angry things get lodged in our heart when we do not really know we are angry we maintain our cool we do not allow ourselves to get angry memory usually do not know what's in their heart I'm OK but wives could tell we have carried bitterness along time when things are lodged in the heart you cannot forgive only Jesus can cleanse the heart

let us draw near with a true heart in full assurance of faith, having our hearts sprinkled from an evil conscience and our bodies washed with pure water. [Hebrews 10:22 (NKJV)]

In our flesh we cannot forgive you cannot get at your heart and make it forgive forgiveness is a work of grace by God there are how do we know if there is something that we have not forgiven?

Typical problems that indicate a buried root are:

- Chronic Illnesses with no physiological diagnosis
- Unwarranted anger
- A certain type of person we do not like
- One of your children really gets under your skin

If you identify with any of these symptoms, pray and ask the Lord to reveal to you the source or root of the issue. It is often most effective to have someone else pray with you. The prayer does not have to be elaborate, a simple prayer like,

"Lord, show me the root of my problem," or

"Lord help."

Often, the Lord will communicate with you as a word, a thought, a dream, or some other means to tell or show you the root problem.

Then you must deal with the problem. This may be the most difficult to accomplish, but the most important thing you can do. Pick up your cross and carry it.

You may need to forgive in order to fully solve your issue. (see Chapter17)

Chapter 10 - Love Others

By this we know love, because He laid down His life for us. And we also ought to lay down our lives for the brethren.[36]

St. John, the evangelist, and theologian was the only one of Jesus' original disciples that lived to a ripe old age and died of natural causes. Towards the end of the first century, when John was near death, his followers gathered in his room and asked if he had any last words to pass on to them. According to church historian, Eusebius, John replied,

"Little children, Love one another." He repeated it over and over again.

Then some asked him, *"Is that all you have to say?"*

"It is enough," John was said to reply, "for *it is the Lord's command."*

There is a common misunderstanding about love that is popular in our post-modern era. There is a misconception that if you genuinely love someone, you must accept everything they do and allow them to do whatever they want. If you disagree with them, it means you not only don't love them, but you hate them.

Our working definition for love is "giving to someone beyond what we get in return." That means putting the other's needs ahead of our own. That includes protecting them from themselves. Loving someone does not mean you allow them a free license to do whatever they want. Love may require imposing restrictions. Loving means we must make decisions regarding the other person's wellbeing if they do not make the right choices.

A loving mother would not allow her child to sit in the middle of a busy street and play because she knows the danger the child could face. If we love someone, we cannot allow them to do whatever they desire. We would put their welfare first and make decisions to prevent them from hurting themselves.

The scribes and Pharisees were always throwing out questions designed to trap Jesus in a conundrum, He could not answer. One day, a certain lawyer tried to test Him by asking,[37] *"What shall I do to inherit eternal Life"*

In typical Rabbinic style, Jesus answered the question with a question of His own, *"What is written in the law? What is your reading of it?"*

The lawyer answered, *"You shall love the LORD your God with all your heart, with all your soul, with all your strength, and with all your mind, and your neighbor as yourself."*

Jesus said to him, *"You have answered rightly; do this and you will live."*

But he, wanting to justify himself, said to Jesus, *"And who is my neighbor?"*

We might ask the same question, *"Who is this neighbor that I am to love as much as I love myself?"*

Jesus responded to the Pharisee with the Parable of the Good Samaritan, in which certain religious people react contrary to love, but not contrary to the expectations of the lawyer.

Ritual cleanliness was a priority for religious Jews. Pharisees, Sadducees, and other religious leaders would go to extremes to avoid becoming unclean, such as touching a wounded man lying in a ditch. They would expect a layperson to come along and help the man. Instead, a Samaritan came by, saw the injured man, and took pity on him. He treated the wounds with oil and wine, bandaged them, put the man on his donkey, and delivered him to a nearby inn. The next day he paid for two months room and board, instructed the innkeeper to take care of the man's needs, and said he would be back to pay for it all.

After sharing this parable, Jesus asked the lawyer, *"Which of these three do you think proved to be a neighbor to the man who fell into the robbers' hands?[38]"*

Note that Jesus reversed the emphasis of the original question. He replaced, *"Who is my neighbor?"* with, *"Who proved to be a neighbor."* Jesus changed the question from the passive form to an active form.

The expert in the law replied, *"The one who had mercy on him."*

Jesus told him, *"Go and do likewise."*

Let's put this parable into a modern perspective.

Around midnight, a man was on his way into a large city, driving along a major highway when he was pulled over, beaten and carjacked by a group of thugs. They took his car and all of his money and threw him in a ditch to die.

Several people passed by but did not want to get involved.

A Democrat said, *"I feel your pain in the ditch."*

A Republican said, *"Only bad people fall into ditches."*

A religious fundamentalist said, *"You deserve the ditch."*

A self-pitying person said, *"You haven't seen anything until you've seen my* ditch."

Then along came a wealthy foreigner returning from a night out gambling and partying in the city. He saw the man and stopped. He tore his own silk shirt and made bandages for the man's wounds, poured whiskey out of his flask to sterilize the wounds, gave him some Tylenol, put him in the front seat of his Cadillac and drove him to the nearest Holiday Inn. There he paid the night manager $3,800 to feed and house the man for a month. The next morning, he left but told the manager to take care of the man's needs and if he owed more, he would be back to pay.

Which of these do you think was a neighbor to the man who fell into the hands of the thugs?

What are we supposed to do?

"Go and do likewise."

Our problem is not normally a lack of compassion, it is more a fear of becoming involved. We are too busy with our own life to take on new burdens from others. If it were someone we knew, say a next-door neighbor in the ditch, we would jump to help without question.

But as Jesus teaches us, our neighbor is not just the folks next door. Our neighbors are the hungry, the needy, the prisoners, hurting people, our friends, and those who hate us. We live in a difficult world, wars, riots, murders, gangs, drugs, domestic violence, and human trafficking. Ministry to those people can become rather messy and time consuming.

When we are faced with the enormous problems of the world, we are must decide what to do. There are two natural tendencies, either we realize the problem is too big and do nothing, or we jump in and try to do everything and quickly burn out. Neither of these are practical. The answer to the "Too Big to Handle" is to find out what part of the problem God wants us to work and then acting on His call. He will place a burden on your heart and show you what to do. When you pray and ask the Lord for direction, the Holy Spirit will lead you.

Many years ago, pastor and author, Steve Sjogren[39], pioneered a program, he termed "Servant Evangelism," which incorporated a unique approach to sharing God's love in practical ways. Steve mobilized his church to go outside of the building and perform random acts of kindness as a living parable demonstrating the love of God, freely given. Since that time, thousands of believers have been deployed into the streets, sharing God's love in practical ways. We first became involved when Steve led us to go door to door, giving away free light bulbs.

Later we began to show God's love in other ways, like standing outside of a supermarket, on a hot summer day, handing out free, ice cold cans of Coca Cola. We did not ask if someone wanted one, we only asked if they wanted diet or regular.

Under the pull tab, we left a card which read, "We hope this small gift refreshes you. It is our way of saying, 'God loves you, no strings attached.'"

The very first person that received a soda from me was a rather large lady with an overflowing shopping cart. Wary of some ulterior motive on our part, she grabbed the can without a word and stalked hurriedly to her car. I watched as she placed the Coke on the roof of her car and loaded the groceries in the back seat. After she finished, she took the coke and got in the car. Then she picked up the card and read our message. After a couple of minutes, she got out of the car and came back to us, clutching the little card in her hand.

In tears, she held up the card and said, *"You do not know what this means to me, but last year, I lost a child and have been angry at God ever since. Lately, I have been feeling that I need to start going back to church. Because of what you have given me, I now know that God does love me, and I have to get back in relationship with Him. Thank you."*

That hooked me on this kind of ministry, and we have continued it in the churches we have served.

The product of performing random acts of kindness is complex. Sharing God's love in practical ways impacts the lives of many of those on the receiving end, but there is an even a more profound effect on those who give. The people receiving the random acts of kindness, may or may not visit the church that gave them the gift, most do not. But those who go out into the neighborhoods and give of themselves are truly transformed and become excited about serving and their enthusiasm is contagious.

It is interesting that not all people are able to receive something free. Approximately ten percent of the people we approach want to give us something in return. If we accept their offer, we reinforce their idea that love is conditional. Performing loving acts of kindness without looking for anything in return boosts our love for others.

There are many people and organizations that feed the poor, visit the sick and prisoners, and perform random acts of kindness out of compassion for those in need. That is all well and good, but I do not want people to look to me, or the government as their source, but to the Lord.

When we share the love of Jesus through acts of love, we are lifting the Lord and encouraging people to seek Him. Introducing people to a loving God will transform their life, not just help them through a difficult time.

On my first trip to India, I was appalled at what I saw in Mumbai. Over three million homeless people live on the streets and sleep under viaducts. Early in the morning, we watched trucks come by to pick up those that had not made it through the night.

With over a billion citizens, India is the world's largest democracy. It has strong social programs, national health care, free schools, and strong labor unions. When I realized the extreme poverty in the middle of a social democracy, I prayed and questioned the Lord,

"Why is there such poverty and despair in such a progressive country?"

The response was, *"It is because they do not know Me, they have no hope."*

When there is no hope, people just give up trying. My heart skipped a beat when I considered the possibility that God might be calling me to be a missionary to India. While I loved the country, the people, and the food, there are other places I would much rather live. The Lord did not call me to that mission but did want me to share the things I saw and experienced.

The late Donald McGavran (1897-1990), missiologist and father of the modern church growth movement, famously noted a correlation between the spread of Christianity and an increase in personal wellbeing - physically, morally, and economically. This is not meant as a nod to the so-called "Prosperity Gospel," but an understanding that a belief in Jesus Christ provides a bridge to God, resulting in what was missing in India's lower castes - <u>hope</u>. Hinduism, the prevalent religion in India, has thousands of gods, and each one demands something from the adherent.

In James Michener's great book, "The Source," he portrays a scene from the town of Makor in the year 2205 BCE. Urbaal and one of his wives Timna, after trying for three years they finally have a son. Then the town Makor is threatened with an attack. A sacrifice of the first-born son must be made to their gods. Urbaal and Timna's child is chosen. Urbaal is happy. Timna is devastated. Urbaal argues with Timna, that he had already surrendered three of his other first-born children by other wives, and they each got over it. Only a few days later we see Urbaal entering a contest to see who would get to spend a week with a temple prostitute. Urbaal wins. In the midst of her agony over losing her only child, when she really needs her husband, he spends a week with the temple prostitute. Timna thinks, *"With different gods, her husband would have been a different man."*

The kind of God we worship determines what kind of person we become, of what behavior we approve, and how we relate to others. Throughout North America and Europe, where Christianity has flourished, there are still many of our neighbors who worship the gods of money, power, drugs, alcohol, the government, relationships, and themselves.

Sharing a loving God with our neighbors is an act of love, and as you do this, you will grow in your love for them.

Unfortunately, if we dislike or hate someone because of their sin, religion, or politics, we will grow in hatred towards them. It is okay to hate sin, but it is not okay to hate the sinner.

Christian love involves giving to others out of the greater love we have received from God. We love because He first loved us. When we are secure in God's love, we can ourselves, and when we love ourselves we are free to love others. Much of our own healing occurs when we decide to love others and show that divine, Godly love through the power and fruit of the Holy Spirit.

Chapter 11 - Love Hurts

"Does it hurt?" asked the rabbit.
"Sometimes," said the skin horse, for he was always truthful. "When you
are real you don't mind being hurt.[40]"

In her children's book, 'The Velveteen Rabbit." Marjery Williams
describes a mythical conversation between a toy rabbit and a toy horse,
while no one else is around.

> *"What is real?" asked the rabbit one day, when they were lying*
> *side by side near the nursery feeder, before Nana came to clean*
> *up the room. "Does it mean having things that buzz inside you*
> *and a stick-out handle?"*

> *"Real isn't how you are made," said the skin horse. "it's a thing*
> *that happens to you. When a child loves you for a long, long*
> *time, not just to play with, but REALLY loves you, then you*
> *become real."*

> *"Does it hurt?" asked the rabbit.*

> *"Sometimes," said the skin horse, for he was always truthful.*
> *"When you are real you don't mind being hurt."*

If we do not care about others, they will not often hurt us. When
we put on our masks and pretend that we are someone else, it does not
hurt as much because we can blame their rejection on our false face. It
is when we become real, that we are most vulnerable.

Becoming real is the single most important objective we must
achieve if we want to genuinely love. To become real, one must learn to
love oneself. When you are real, you come out from behind the facade,
and you become vulnerable and open yourself up to the real possibility
of being hurt. In loving another, we choose to become vulnerable,

because real love does not exist when hiding behind our protective barriers.

When I was ten years old, we visited a lapidarist; an artist who uses the lapidary techniques of cutting, grinding, and polishing stone, minerals, or gemstones into decorative items. Two things stood out to me in his basement workshop. First, he had an ultraviolet lamp which in the dark caused certain minerals to glow brightly, and then there was the rock tumbler. The tumbler was used to transform rough rocks into smooth polished stones. You first half-fill a cylindrical tumbler with rocks and turn on the motor which rotates the cylinder, tumbling the rocks. As they pummel one another, they knock sharp edges off. After three to seven days of tumbling, the rocks become smooth. Grit is then added to further irritate the stones, polishing them to a smoother surface. That is what God does for us.

Our life here on earth is our rock tumbler. Sharp edges are knocked off by bumping against others and facing pain. If we avoid this difficult process, we cannot grow in love.

We are hurt by others when their deception is revealed, when we they reject us, or when they leave us. It is normal for loved ones, whose love we relied upon, to one day be gone. Sometimes friends move away, and our parents grow old and pass on. As we age, we note the passing of close friends and family members preceding us in death. But we seldom think about our children going before us, although that also may occur.

Mary, the mother of Jesus, witnessed her Beloved Son, being tortured, tied to a tree, and die before her very eyes. She may or may not have anticipated His resurrection, but that did not salve the hurt of watching Him suffer.

No matter the reason, hurt is overwhelming. There is no way that we can escape the pain caused by a loved one's deception, rejection, or departure. By loving them, we made ourselves vulnerable. We opened ourselves up because of our need and desire for love.

There is an alternative to becoming vulnerable, but in the end, it is far more painful. Instead of opening ourselves up, we can choose to close ourselves up and develop a "Heart of Stone." Often, this will keep most people far away.

The Heart of Stone is a defense mechanism that we build around our emotional center, our heart, to protect it from hurt. It is a wall we build in hopes of eliminating the pain of rejection. When that wall is set in place, we become like zombies; living, breathing, and going through the physical activities of life, but our heart and soul are without essence. When our wall is threatened, we react in fear and act to preserve our security. With the wall firmly in place, relationships never progress beyond the superficial.

Pain from loving pummels us and transforms our heart of stone into a heart of flesh.

There are two kinds of hearts of stone. The first kind is obvious; it is the hard-hearted person who does not care about anyone or anything except themselves. We say, "His heart is so hard he will never help."

The second kind is less obvious. It is the hidden heart of stone. People with the hidden heart of stone will act loving and will be ready to help others. They may act loving and outgoing but will never let anyone know what is in their own heart. They fear intimacy. They will not let anyone get close enough to hurt them. When a relationship begins to deepen, they will deliberately do something mean to drive the other person away. They are prone to fall into sexual sin because they are afraid to express their feelings.

"Pistanthrophobia" is the fear trusting others and it is often the result of experiencing a serious disappointment or painful ending to a prior relationship. The fear of vulnerability is ultimately a fear of rejection or abandonment.

It was many years into our marriage when I learned about my hidden heart of stone. It was while attending a workshop led by John Sandford.[41]

I was content to live behind my defenses for decades, until I met Rita. On our first date, I realized that this could never be a superficial relationship. My normal reaction would have been to break with her immediately, but there was also a hope that this could lead to real love.

For the next month, I struggled with the decision. Was I willing to take a chance? Continuing to date would result in the removal of some stones in my wall and I could become vulnerable. A month later, after deciding that the potential reward was worth the risk, we had our second date.

Six happy months later we were married, but unfortunately, my walls were still intact. As we honeymooned in Ocho Rios, Jamaica, my walls began to crumble under the weight of Rita's love. Feeling vulnerable, panic set in. At first, I stuffed the fear, and toughened it out through that ominous sense of impending danger, as I had in years past.

Then one day the stuffed-up fear, erupted in a totally unwarranted, outburst of anger. It was way out of context and pushed Rita away, temporarily removing the threat to my wall and my vulnerability. While I hated how I reacted, and what it did to Rita, I felt safer.

You have been hurt before, so you seek to minimize the risk of being hurt again. However, the best way to minimize the potential damage is not to build walls or try to act according to some self-created checklist. Instead, the solution is counter intuitive. To combat the fear of vulnerability, you must first learn to love and accept your whole, authentic self. Loving ourselves is one of the toughest lessons we will ever face. We all have flaws, imperfections, embarrassing stories, and past mistakes we wish we could forget. We are insecure, awkward, and desperately wishing we could change certain things. That's human nature.[42]»

The first century Church in Corinth had serious problems that the apostle, Paul had to deal with. Much of it was caused by their inability to be honest with each other and with St. Paul. In his second epistle, Paul points this out.

"O Corinthians! We have spoken openly to you, our heart is wide open. You are not restricted by us, but you are restricted by your own affections. Now in return for the same (I speak as to children), you also be open.[43]

When you have been hurt, it is nearly impossible to be open and vulnerable, because nobody wants to go through the pain again.

In the Eastern Orthodox Christian Church, bishops and priests prepare themselves for the Divine Liturgy, (Holy Communion) by praying through a specific liturgy, called the "Kairon." To prepare, bless, and serve communion, the communicant is required to maintain his relationship with the Lord. Any defensive walls between the man and God, can break that bond. In this liturgy, the priest or bishop will pray that he, and all others, lay aside all defenses to be fully open to God.

Have mercy on us, O Lord, have mercy on us; for laying aside all defense we sinners offer unto Thee, as Master, this supplication: have mercy on us.[48]

Becoming vulnerable is a prerequisite to being able to love someone with abandon.

Chapter 12 - Love with Abandon

"The future we face at the dawn of the twenty-first century is, like all futures left to themselves, "emergent, complex messiness." Its "messiness" lies not in disorder, but in an order that is unpredictable, spontaneous, and ever shifting, a pattern created by millions of uncoordinated, independent decisions.[49]
[Virginia Postrel - The Future and Its enemies]

To me, there is nothing more exciting than a newly saved Christian. They are vibrant, enthusiastic, and madly in love with Jesus. Suddenly free of the condemnation of past sins, they are bursting with enthusiasm and want to share their new-found salvation with anyone who might listen.

Unfortunately, in six to twelve months, that initial enthusiasm wanes as some in the church step in to explain the rules and enforce the rules.

In her timely book "The Future and Its Enemies," author Virginia Postrel wrote that a major battle was forming for the future of the nation, not between opposing tribes, liberals and conservatives, nor even between nations, but between "Dynamists" and "Stasists." She went on to define a "dynamist" as one who sees change as an evolution through variation, feedback, and adaptation or more simply, trial-and-error. Dynamists are not afraid to make mistakes because they grow from their errors. There is spontaneity and wild abandon in dynamism. Creativity flourishes in a dynamist environment.

Stasists, on the other hand, feel that they must control progress by establishing rules and regulations to ensure safety and avoid mistakes. We see churches and government agencies establishing rules and regulations to make sure people do not make mistakes, but they inhibit creativity and growth.

In the church, the Stasists are the Pharisees and religious police. Some rules are important, but Christianity is a different kind of religion. It has always been concerned more about knowing and following Christ, than following the rules of the Church.

> *"God dwells in a state of perpetual enthusiasm. He is delighted with all that is good and lovingly concerned about all that is wrong. He pursues His labors always in a fullness of holy zeal. No wonder the Spirit came at Pentecost as a sound of a rushing wind and sat in tongues of fire on every forehead... Whatever else happened at Pentecost, one thing that cannot be missed by the most casual observer was the sudden upsurging of moral enthusiasm. Those first disciples burned with a steady, inward fire. They were enthusiastic to the point of complete abandon.*
> *[A. W. Tozer[50]]*

Mistakes are the consequences of complete abandon, but they are also signs of life and growth. When our daughter, Rhonda, was eight, we bought her a pair of roller skates. Immediately she ran to the carport to try to skate. She had not skated before but had watched her friends and believed she could skate. My wife Rita watched carefully as Rhonda took her first hesitant, tottering steps, then scrambled to maintain balance. Each time it appeared she would fall; Rita was out the door ready to catch her.

After watching this scenario play through several times, I told Rita, *"Let her fall. It is OK. That's the way she will learn to skate."*

That may sound cruel, and it wasn't appreciated at the time, but in falling we learn to stand up. That is how an infant learns to walk, by trying and failing.

That is also how we learn to love, by trying and failing. Learning to walk, roller skate, or love another will result in bruises. You will not learn to love unless you have been hurt.

The late John Wimber, leader of the Vineyard Church Movement and what church historians term, "The Third Wave of The Holy Spirit," often declared that he never trusted a leader who did not walk with a limp.

If you are protected from the consequences of your mistakes you will not learn as fast or as well.

If you need a biblical example, look at Peter. Jesus could have prevented Peter from denying Him three times. He did warn him that Satan would test him, but Jesus prayed that after Peter fell, he would return, and his experience would strengthen him and the other disciples.[51]

In the mid-twentieth century there was a phenomenon in Africa as missionaries from England and the United States presented the Gospel to indigenous peoples with powerful results. Many of the new converts, after hearing the Good News, returned to their villages in the bush and shared what they had learned with their village. Thousands of new "Mushroom Churches" began to spring up in the interior as these natives now on-fire for God held meetings. They simply shared their excitement and what they knew.

When the mission boards back home heard about these native evangelists, they were less than pleased by the news, and tried to shut the churches down because the natives, sharing their joy, were not seminary educated.[52]

John, the beloved apostle, was in exile on the Island of Patmos when Jesus came to him in a vision and instructed him to write letters to seven of the churches in Asia. One of those letters was addressed to the Church at Laodicea, where Jesus instructed John to tell them:

> *"I know your deeds, that you are neither cold nor hot. I wish*
> *you were either one or the other! So, because you are lukewarm*
> *- neither hot nor cold - I am about to spit you out of my mouth.*
> *[Rev. 3:15-16]"*

The Laodiceans, just like many believers today, had lost their love for Jesus. The church in Laodicea reflected the city, which was quite prosperous, and from all outward appearances seemed to be in excellent condition. But it was an example of a nominal, self-satisfied, form of Christianity. Permeated with complacency, it lacked power and passion. No one thing stood out; there were no excesses nor notable achievements. They had learned to compromise and accommodate themselves to the needs of the world. They did not take a stand for anything. Their problem was not a lack of religion, but a lack of a knowing and loving Jesus Christ. There was no personal relationship. The main issue was not indifference, but ignorance of their condition. They were clueless and what is more, they did not care.

Jesus calls their attention to their true spiritual condition, which is wretched and pitied by God. He tells them they are poor, blind, and naked - referring to their need for that authentic love relationship with Jesus Christ. Despite their problems, Christ still loves them, as He reveals their condition, disciplines them, and calls them to repentance.

As a child growing up in suburban Chicago, all my friends had a nickname. Mine was "Wild Bill," because I would try anything once - just like Mikie in the breakfast food commercials. Down the street from my house were three tall elm trees. This was where we learned to climb. One day I a couple of squirrels playing follow the leader in the trees, I watched them go out on a limb of one tree and jump across to a branch on the adjacent tree. The thought came to me, "That looks like fun, I'll bet I can do that."

My planning was detailed. I analyzed the distance I would need to jump and the strength of the branches. Finding a limb strong enough to support my eighty-five-pound frame to get me within eight feet of a limb on the next tree, I set my plan in motion and stepped gingerly out from the trunk. This was going to be easier than I originally thought. The branch in the opposite tree was waiting for me a short eight-foot leap away. It was now or never. I leapt. Unfortunately my calculations did not take into account the flexibility of the limb from which I would launch and I flew a foot short of my target, falling to the ground below tightly grasping leaves and skinny branches off of the target tree. They slowed my descent enough to prevent more serious injury. Sitting on the ground with a bruised ego and tail bone, I thought, "It could have been worse. Someone might have been watching.

In my mind I will always want to make that leap again and prove that it can be done, but the memory of the pain has kept me from another attempt.

Getting hurt will make one cautious. If we have been hurt in seeking love, we often stop seeking. If you are hurt often enough, you may give up and not want to try anymore. When we love, we make ourselves vulnerable to being hurt.

When we love someone with all our heart, soul, mind, and strength we are vulnerable to the object of our love, who can hurt us.

The Early Church was wild. They loved God with all their heart, soul, mind, and strength. They lived in wild abandon, trusting Him for all their needs. They expected Him to act on their behalf. They prayed and saw people healed. They raised people from the dead on a regular basis. Tradition tells us that Andrew, the brother of Peter, was strolling along the seashore and came upon a tragic shipwreck, and the bodies of two hundred dead sailors had washed up on the shore. Overcome with sadness and compassion, Andrew prayed and asked God to raise all of them from the dead, and God obliged.

The church grew through the persecutions and martyrdom of wild martyrs who abandoned their fear of torture and death, speaking out for the cause of Christ.

This wild abandonment for God did not last. When the church became safer and more respectable and many of the wild ones moved out to the deserts of Egypt and Arabia where they could follow Christ with wild abandon.

Today, much of the Church has become "Functional Atheists." That is, they believe in God, but live their lives as if God did not exist. A functional atheist is afraid to make a full commitment to God's leadership. They may regularly attend church but do not expect God to show up. They believe God can heal, but do not expect Him to do it for them. They may have God as their co-pilot, but never allow Him to take the controls. They rely on their own logic rather than the Holy Spirit. These are Christians in name only. They try to live the Christian life, but their life is dull and without fire or power.

"... if the Holy Spirit were completely removed from the world today, 90% of the work of the church would go on as if nothing at all had happened." - [R. T. Kendall]

Still, every generation has had wild ones in the church.

My fear is not that our great movement, known as the Methodists, will eventually cease to exist or one day die from the earth. My fear is that our people will become content to live without the fire, the power, the excitement, the supernatural element that makes us great. [John Wesley]

"The great sin of church is not that we've lost the power of God, but that we've become content to live without it." - [Charles Finney]

The United States of America was founded by "Wild Ones." They had a national theology based upon Israel, a chosen nation established as God's theocracy to shine God's light to the world - to lead people to life, liberty, and the pursuit of happiness. Now they are apologizing for believing in the one true God.

Do you really love God or is He just an abstract being? If we really love God, then we would pursue Him with a wild abandon - Nothing else in life would be as important.

When Jesus called Peter, Andrew, James, John, and even Matthew, these working-class men abandoned their careers, their plans for the future, and their families to follow Him.

After they had been with Him for a while Jesus told them,

> *"If anyone desires to come after Me, let him deny himself, and take up his cross, and follow Me. For whoever desires to save his life will lose it, but whoever loses his life for My sake will find it. [Matthew 16:24-25 (NKJV)]*

We must go for it! Taste the new wine of a life that defies the law of gravity, a life which throws caution to the wind, where danger and risk await. Abandon yourself to the one who will never abandon you.

Most of us have lost touch with the childlike experience of "abandon." We believe in Jesus. We love the idea of Jesus. We try to do what we believe He wants us to do, but abandon everything, job, security, home, our parent's expectations, our future? That sounds scary.

Abandon is unpredictable. We cannot have people running around discarding responsible behavior in the name of Jesus. After all, every society must have rules. Rules are structures that protect us from anarchy. Rules and laws protect society from chaos and confusion. We cannot have people breaking the rules in the name of Jesus, can we?

Yes, we can. It means allowing The Holy Spirit to Guide us. We have conditioned ourselves to allow our mind, will, and emotions to control our actions. God wants us to be controlled by the Holy Spirit.

If we truly love Jesus with all our heart, soul, mind and strength, we must be willing to abandon our agenda, our schedules, our favorite things, our security, our need for certainty, our fear of making mistakes, and the expectations of others.

A life of loving Jesus is a life of resistance, a lonely life, a minority life, and some people will never understand. But it is an exciting, abundant life that God promises. It is the Kingdom of God, the Pearl of Great Price, and the treasure buried in the field. We all wish that we could love like that, but do not feel that it is in our future.

It is not politically correct to love God with all our heart, soul, mind, and strength. It may be alright to read about God, but do not become a fanatic. People seriously in love with God are accused of being psychotic.

So, how can we move away from our past hurts and fears to allow ourselves to become that vulnerability? The rewards of loving with abandon are many. You will be able to take chances because you will not fear failure. You will be able leap like the squirrels, roller skate with the best, and love without fear.

When we live our life in fear, we are not alive.

When you fail, you may get hurt, but it will not be fatal.

Then you can, *"pick yourself up, brush yourself off, and start all over again."*[53]

Chapter 13 - Become a Lover

Beloved, let us love one another, for love is of God; and everyone who loves is born of God and knows God. He who does not love does not know God, for God is love. [1 John 4:7-8 (NKJV)]

Christian author and theologian, Leonard Sweet[54] describes the times we live in as the TGIF era. (Twitter, Google, I-Phone, and Face Book.) Sweet marks the beginning of this age as 1973 when Martin Cooper and his team from the Motorola Corporation invented the cell phone. Those born after 1973, Sweet identifies as "Googlers" while those born prior to the invention of the cell phone he refers to as "Gutenbergers." Gutenbergers grew up reading printed books. Print information is expensive to publish and distribute. Googlers on the other hand grew up with the Internet and its volumes of free information.

Our world has become knowledge based. There has been an explosion of knowledge for the past decades. Most of what we know today did not exist ten years ago. Just look at what we have learned recently about viruses.

Three thousand years ago, knowledge traveled at the speed of a messenger on foot. Two hundred years ago, at the time of George Washington and the founding of the United States of America, knowledge still traveled at the speed of a foot messenger. Today knowledge travels at the speed of light. Whatever you want to know can be found instantaneously.

If you want to know how to build a house, milk a cow, or replace a grommet, you can find a video on You-Tube to show you. Almost anything you want to know you can find somewhere on the Internet.

This is surely the end-times prophesied by Daniel.[55]

You can learn about love, sex, marriage, and other people's foibles, but knowledge about love will not make you a lover nor transform your life. By the way, do not Google "love," there are some things you will not want to see on-line.

You can read all you want to know about love, but knowledge alone will not make you a lover. If you want to become a lover, to love rightly, and receive love, a source of genuine love must transform your life. Our ability to love others is rooted in our finding and securing a real, unfailing love for ourselves.

The only way we can become secure in love is through being loved, and not just any love will do. We need a powerful and persistent source of love. We need a source of love that is strong enough to break through our broken, wounded, and sinful state. We need the love of God.

A Christian is not a Christian simply because he is able to talk about God, he is a Christian because he is able to have experience of God. Just as when you really love someone and converse with them you feel their presence and you enjoy this presence, so it happens in man's communion with God. There exists not a simple external relationship but a mystical union of God and man in the Holy Spirit

Knowledge may tell us what we are looking for, but it will not transform our heart. It is not about learning; it is all about becoming.

The love of God must be the engine that changes our hearts.

"I will give you a new heart and put a new spirit within you; I will take the heart of stone out of your flesh and give you a heart of flesh."[Ezekiel 36:26 (NKJV)]

The "heart of stone" results from emotional hurts which build up over the years and cause us to set up defensive walls. A hard heart often manifests as not caring about anyone or anything except himself.

Another form of the heart of stone is less obvious. It is the hidden heart of stone. With the hidden heart of stone, a person may act loving, may even be always ready to help others, but they will not let anyone help them. They will act extremely loving and outgoing but will let no one know what is in their own heart. They need to be in control.

Those with this hidden heart of stone fear intimacy. They will not let anyone get close enough to hurt them. When a relationship grows intimate, they will deliberately do something mean to drive the other person away. Those with the hidden heart of stone are prone to fall into sexual sin because they are often covering up feelings, they are afraid to express.

Knowledge about love cannot remove the heart of stone. The only way to receive your heart transplant is to experience that unfailing, unconditional, and prodigal love of God.

When Jesus first called Peter, Andrew, and the sons of Zebedee, He told them He would make them fishers of men. Notice what Jesus did not say, "*I will __teach__ you how to fish for men.*"

He said when you follow Me, I will __*make*__ you fishers of men.

In our search for love, it is not about learning how to love. It is about following Jesus and by following Him, experiencing His love, then we will be like Him and become lovers.

Seventeenth century French writer, theologian, and inventor Blaise Pascal described this need for God as an infinite abyss in the human soul.

> *"the infinite abyss can only be filled by an infinite and immutable object, that is to say, only by God Himself.*[56]*"*
> *[Blaise Pascal]*

That hole inside of us can only be filled by God, who is love.

We need His love to first shine on us.

If God is love, and we mortals barely grasp the concept of the God who is love, how can we understand love itself. Jesus is God, the second person of the Trinity, and we have the Gospel accounts of His life and ministry to show us love.

Since we were little children we sang "Jesus Loves me this I know," but for many it has been difficult to realize that God the Father also loves us. But it was God, the Father who sent His only begotten Son into our world, to die that we might have eternal life with Him. God, who is love, loves us with the same love and same intensity that He Loves His Son Jesus.[57]

Jesus died on the cross and rose from the dead to secure us in love. We behold His act of love on the cross and allow its power to change our hearts. The cross reveals the unchanging truth that God loves us and reveals to us that God's love is more powerful than what we call love. It proclaims to us that nothing can separate us from God's love.

1 John 4:10 This is love: not that we loved God, but that he loved us and sent his Son as an atoning sacrifice for our sins.

Romans 5:5 And hope does not disappoint us, because God has poured out his love into our hearts by the Holy Spirit, whom he has given us.

Jesus reveals to us the Father's love.

While very rarely someone might die for a great and righteous person, Jesus died for us while we were sinners in rebellion against God.[Romans 5:7-8]

Romans 8:38-39 For I am convinced that neither death nor life, neither angels nor demons, neither the present nor the future, nor any powers, [39] neither height nor depth, nor anything else in all creation, will be able to separate us from the love of God that is in Christ Jesus our Lord.

God wants us to know His Father's heart of love, revealed in Jesus. He wants to win us over to this sweet and powerful love. We will not be secure in love until we can receive God's love.

Many of us struggle with God as Father because of our many inadequate and distorted human images of "father love." But we all need a father. It is in our fathers we find our identity, confidence, values, and an understanding of our purpose in life. Children cry out for the healing touch of a loving father. When it is not forthcoming, children, teens, and adults search for something to fill that emptiness. Without a loving father they have no confidence, they wander around without purpose nor identity. Doubting their abilities, they feel rejected. Cultural father-less-ness leads to prodigal lifestyles.

It is hard to accept that God the Father loves you and to trust Him if you did not have a good relationship with your earthly father. If this is the case, we must deal with these issues if we are to fully receive God's love. That requires forgiveness of of those whose love was not adequate.

Many of us have experienced problems with earthly fathers, furious exchanges, physical or verbal abuse, and rejection. God, the Father wants us to know, at the deepest level of our heart, that we are accepted and loved by Him. Through Jesus Christ, we have become His own sons and daughters. The Holy Spirit testifies with our spirit that we are His children. [58]

In high school, my father only came to one of my football games. That day, I played like a man possessed. I wanted to impress him. At a very crucial point in the game, I made a great play tackling a powerful runner to save a touchdown. Making a diving tackle, something in my shoulder snapped, and I was slow to get up. My teammates praised me as I had to leave the game, but later, my father accused me later of faking an injury. It devastated me. Most of all, I so wanted to please him.

My father never disciplined me - It was always my mother. His untimely death, while I was in college, left me with the feeling of being abandoned and empty. To fill that emptiness, I tried many things, religion, alcohol, danger, and wrong relationships. This continued for the next ten years. It was not until I met and married Rita that I moved back to a healthier and happier path.

Sometime later, at a Christian retreat, the leader asked us to make an evaluation of our relationship with God. We were to go to the chapel, pray, and ask the Lord about our relationship. I was highly active in our church, was in lay ministry, and felt a strong call into full-time ministry. I thought I was in a great place - with the Lord. Expecting a comfortable time of prayer, I knelt in a pew back in a far corner of the chapel.

My prayer began, *"Dear Lord, we do have a great relationship, don't we?"*

I waited in anticipation for some response, a warm feeling, an assuring word, or a sense of peace in my spirit. But there was nothing but the darkness of the chapel. Only a single candle burned on the altar thirty feet away.

"Lord, aren't we good?"

Still nothing. I became anxious and panicked. It like God had disappeared or turned His back on me. I felt completely alone, abandoned, and cold.

"Help me, Lord, what is happening?"

A movie played in my mind. I had climbed up this big oak tree and was walking out on a large limb. Moving further out, I looked back at the trunk and watched as a huge chainsaw began to cut through the very limb on which I stood. Then I heard these words in my spirit,

"You do not trust Me."

It was true. God was calling me to follow Him, and I had partially responded, but was afraid to commit completely to His leadership of my life. Somewhere deep in my heart was the fear that I could not trust Him. I had to have a back-up plan. Going out on a limb for God was too scary, He might cut it off and I could fall and get hurt. Where did this fear originate? Then another incident came to mind. My father and I were working together in the vegetable garden. He and mother had had a big fight, and he told me he was going to leave us. I begged him to take me with him, but he refused. He did not leave, but that moment had stuck with me. He left at another time but returned. Then while I was in college when I needed him most, he died, and was gone for good.

Without trust, it is almost impossible to love freely. Without faith you are not free to love, because genuine love requires a vulnerability. You cannot fully give of yourself when you are worried about being hurt.

The author of the letter to the Hebrews writes that without faith it is impossible to please God.[59] And that faith is a trust that He is God, and that He cares about those who follow Him.

That is what it takes to love God without fear and be able to receive His love. We trust that He is all powerful, always present, and all knowing, Creator of the universe and that He cares for you and me.

St Paul writes in his letter to the Romans,

> *"For you did not receive the spirit of bondage again to fear, but you received the Spirit of adoption by whom we cry out, 'Abba, Father.[60]'"*

In His humanity, Jesus received assurance of His Father's love at critical times in His ministry.

> *Matthew 3:17 And a voice from heaven said, "This is my Son, whom I love; with him I am well pleased."*

Being secure in God's love has amazing benefits. We begin to receive His blessings on our personhood and begin to realize who we really are. We are created in His image, male and female.

Since I did not receive that blessing from my earthly father, I struggled to find security in my identity. I never knew my place, who I was, what I was to become.

Now I have learned to listen to the voice of my heavenly Father. He consistently reminds me of my adequacy as a man. When I am tempted to listen to my own belittling voice, or that of another, all I must do is steal away and recall God's voice which has rung throughout the years.

"This is my Son, whom I love; with him I am well pleased."

When we realize that our father loves us, and He is well pleased with us we can avoid temptation. Out of His affirmation upon our personhood, we can walk uprightly as sons and daughters of honor. When Satan or his minions try to tell us it doesn't matter if we sin or we are no good, we ought to just give up, we don't have to give in to the enemy when we know whose we are.

The Father makes us honorable because He makes us His own. As we go forward in our true status, we reveal the honor that is His very essence. He alone is worthy of all honor, yet He bestows that honor on His sons and daughters. Such an honor causes us to not compromise in our relationships. We are sons and daughters of the King. Secure in our Father's love and His blessing and honor, we grow beyond our old ways of securing love.

Part of our emergence into security in the Father's love involves our response back to Him. We Love others freely from the overflow of love we receive from God. His love is patient, kind, neither boastful nor proud, not self-seeking or readily angered, keeping no record of wrongs. His love protects and hopes for the best in our hearts.

Since God is love, we grow in love by becoming more Christlike.

Chapter 14 - Love's Power

"... inasmuch as you did it to one of the least of these My brethren, you did it to Me."

Until that moment, we had been busy preparing snacks, setting up a hundred chairs in a large circle around the room, and preparing coffee and punch for the guests who would soon arrive. Now we were sitting and waiting. Each of us wore a large cardboard sign hanging on a string from our neck. On it was our first name scrawled in crayon.

An uneasiness, almost panic, griped me. "Can I get out of here now?" but it was too late to run. Being naturally shy, it has always difficult for me to meet new people. Even more to the point, we were all sitting in the visitors center, at the South Mississippi Correctional Facility awaiting fifty inmates with whom we would spend the next three days, sharing meals, listening to talks, praying, and sharing our love. It was my first time inside a prison, and my first time serving on a "KAIROS Prison Ministry" team.

To say that I was intimidated was only a slight overstatement, but the Lord called me to face this challenge. What kept me motivated was Christ's statement in Matthew 25:36 & 40.

"I was in prison and you came to Me...... inasmuch as you did it to one of the least of these My brethren, you did it to Me."

It was an act of obedience on my part. The Lord had been leading me in this direction for several years and now had finally given in. For the past eight weeks, we had become a close-knit team, meeting once a week for several hours, practicing, praying, and worshiping together. We were prepared to serve and share our love, but they did not prepare me for the emotional trip that was coming, nor was I ready for the impact this weekend would have on the rest of my life.

Our team was comprised of fifty men inside the prison, and at least that number of men and women supporting us from a local church where they prepared meals, snacks, and other items designed to show love to our guests living within chain-link fences and barbed wire.

Then came the dreaded moment. Our guests, the inmates, entered the room sporadically. They were coming from different prison units and were not all released at the same time. As each entered the leader announced their name, and one of our team would go forward to greet him. We all had an extra name tag, identical to those we wore, with the name of the man we would host for the next few days. When their name was called, the team member with that name tag would greet their man, serve him some cookies, get him a drink of either punch, tea, or coffee, sit down with him, and get acquainted.

This was be hard for me, because small talk is not my forte, I can never think of what to say. We were instructed not ask about the crime for which they were in prison, nor for how long their sentence.

Suddenly it was my turn. They called out the name on my card, and I went forward and met Jack. He was older than most of the other men, probably in his late sixties, (I guessed) white hair, not much over five feet tall, slightly overweight, Caucasian, and wearing a big smile. He was friendly and outgoing with an unexpected cheerfulness. My fear vanished as he put me at ease. As we headed toward a chair in the big circle, he asked me a question.

"How long do you think I have been in prison?"

Uh oh, this was one question we could not ask.

"I have no idea," I responded hesitatingly.

"Guess."

"Okay, I guess twenty years?"

"No," he responded almost proudly, "I have been in prison fifty-two years."

After serving him cookies and coffee from the food table, I sat down with Jack, and was about to start a new conversation when a large black man walked past and Jack got up, greeted him with a hug, and acted like a long-lost brother who he had not seen in years.

When the man left and went on to his seat, I asked Jack, *"Where do you know him from?"*

"We were on death row together at Parchman," Jack responded.

Parchman is the notorious Mississippi prison where the worst offenders are sent. Jack was in for murder. He was so dangerous that they had sentenced him to death. Here I was serving him, getting to know him, and enjoying his company.

Something inside of me had suddenly changed. I no longer saw Jack as a prison inmate and murderer, although he still is serving a life sentence. Now I saw Jack as a child of God, a man loved by God, who needed to know the love of his heavenly Father. I loved him as a brother. Not agape, where it was my duty as a Christian to love, but phileo, as I felt a connection as a brother. I was experiencing God's love in a whole new form. This transformation took less than fifteen minutes.

It was new, almost instantaneous, and very real. But how did it happen? What was the trigger that transformed me from a tentative, obedient servant into an active, zealous participant? Was it the Holy Spirit in me that made God's love known? Was it getting to know Jack, by sitting down and talking with him, or was it my willingness to set aside my own agenda to serve others?

As I write this today and think back to that moment, decades ago, I realize that it was all that and much more.

C. S. Lewis was right, if you want to love someone, start by doing loving things for them and you will love them.

God even calls us to love our enemies. The Bible tells us to bless those who hurt us. That means we are to pray for many good things to happen to them. To invest ourselves in love for his benefit.

Bless those who persecute you; bless and do not curse. Rejoice with those who rejoice; mourn with those who mourn. Live in harmony with one another. Do not be proud but be willing to associate with people of low position. Do not be conceited. Do not repay anyone evil for evil. Be careful to do what is right in the eyes of everybody. If it is possible, as far as it depends on you, live at peace with everyone. Do not take revenge, my friends, but leave room for God's wrath, for it is written: "It is mine to avenge; I will repay," says the Lord. On the contrary: "If your enemy is hungry, feed him; if he is thirsty, give him something to drink. In doing this, you will heap burning coals on his head." Do not be overcome by evil, but overcome evil with good.[Romans 12:14-21]

There have been many interpretations of this passage and the meaning of the phrase, "heap burning coals on his head."

Some commentators see this as God's wrath to be poured out on the sinner, while the Expositor's Bible Commentary, writes,

"Burning coals" are best understood as "the burning pangs of shame and contrition" (Cranfield, in loc.). There is no definite promise at this point that the offender will be converted, but at least he will not be a threat in the future. Moreover, by going the second mile and showing unexpected and unmerited kindness, the believer may well have spared his companions from having the same experience he has endured. In that measure, society has benefited.

But I like the explanation given to me by an Armenian Pastor who explained that in the Middle East during Biblical times, fire was a precious commodity. People cooked with a fire between two bricks.

One man in each village was appointed as the fire keeper. All night long he kept a fire burning. In the morning he would put a block of wood on his head, then set a brazier of hot coals on top of the block of wood and go house to house, placing a few burning coals in the fireplace of every home, to be for heat and cooking breakfast.

The Armenian pastor told us, *"Heaping burning coals on his head became and idiom in Hebrew, meaning to turn the man into a spreader of warmth in the community.*

Loving and blessing your enemy will transform both you and your enemy into lovers.

Chapter 15 - Love is Listening

So then my beloved brethren, let every man be swift to hear, slow to speak, slow to wrath. [James 1:19]

If you genuinely want to show love to another person, learn how to listen to them.

After over fifty years of marriage, I have learned that when my wife has a problem that she wants to tell me about; she does not want me to fix it for her. She wants me to just listen. Still, I cannot resist the urge to fix her. I want to analyze the problem and propose a solution.

Wrong! She wants to share how she feels and just wants me to listen.

Listening is an act of love; it is one of the greatest acts of love that we can give to another person. It is estimated[61] that in 2020, we will spend over $238 billion for mental health services in the US.

That includes payment to hospitals, psychologists, and psychiatric services, but does not include voluntary services of church and clergy. Much of these costs could be reduced or eliminated by ordinary people who are good listeners.

We all have a story to tell. While writing this book, we have had a pandemic, racial unrest, political intrigue, and an overactive hurricane season. Survivors of catastrophic events have a story to tell and need a place where they can share. Survivors of violence, abuse, and danger all have stories to tell and telling them is cathartic.

Recently I watched an Internet Podcast by a survivor of a recent hurricane. As they described the storm and its aftermath, I listened, but could not help but think about my own experiences of Camile, Katrina, and several other lesser storms.

I kept thinking, *"I'd love to tell him about my dealing with Katrina."* For a moment I considered sending them a comment with my story.

Then I realized what I was doing. Yes I had a story, but this was their story to tell and I must give them the courtesy of listening.

I am sure that survivors of earlier epidemics, when hearing survivors of our recent pandemic share their stories, are anxious to tell their story. Survivors of the Titanic must have been chafing at the bit while listening to the Andrea Doria survivors forty years later telling their stories, and survivors of the Swine Fly pandemic of 2009-2010 which infected over one and a half billion people, want to tell their story while listening to the COVID-19 survivors tell their story.

We do not listen to other people because we are thinking about the story, we want to tell them and waiting for the opportunity to jump in when they slow down or pause for a second.

That reminds me of a story I once heard of a man who survived the Johnstown flood. On Friday, May 31, 1889, there was a catastrophic failure of the South Fork Dam of the Little Conemaugh River, fourteen miles upstream from Johnstown, Pennsylvania which killed over twenty-two hundred people. This survivor always wanted to tell his story of survival, but people kept putting him off. He died seventy-five years later without ever telling his story. When he arrived in heaven, he thinks, *"This is heaven I know I can tell my story here."*

So he talks to Saint Peter who seems to be in charge and Saint Peter says, *"That's wonderful, we have a time where people get to share their stories of bravery and survival and you can tell your story. I'll just check the schedule and plug you in at the next opening."*

Later, Saint Peter comes up to the man and tells him he is on the schedule. *"You are on the schedule to tell of your survival in the Johnstown flood. That's the good news."*

The man stared at Peter with a quizzical look on his face and asked, *"Good news? Is there bad news? What's the bad news?*

Peter responded, *"You will be sharing right after Noah tells his story."*

It is so hard to listen to others while we wait to insert our comments. That is why communications have become so garbled in our modern world. We do not seriously listen, and that is why we fail to get along. Our minds are so busy thinking about what we want to say that it is impossible to hear what others say. When we fail to hear, we often jump to false conclusions. It would be a different world and we would all get along better if we could listen better.

Listening is valuing others. When we listen to others, we give clear evidence that we value what they have to say, and therefore value them.

> *Proverbs 12:15 Fools think their own way is right, but the wise listen to advice (NRSV)*

James, the half-brother of Jesus, tells us to be swift to hear and slow to speak. We must listen more and speak less. How much strife and division could have been prevented if true listening had been practiced instead of hasty speech and voicing impetuous opinions.

> *Romans 12:15-17 "Rejoice with those who rejoice, and weep with those who weep. Be of the same mind toward one another. Do not set your mind on high things, but associate with the humble. Do not be wise in your own opinion. Repay no one evil for evil. Have regard for good things in the sight of all men."*

Humility sensitizes our spiritual hearing, whereas pride dulls our ability to hear.

Wouldn't it be great if we started a ministry of listening, listening without an agenda, listening without trying to tell our story, can we do this? I don't know, but we need to try. The next time your best friend, spouse, child, or parent wants to tell you something, try to listen; without thinking about what you're going to say, without disagreeing, without interrupting, Listen with your mind, listen with your soul, listen with your heart.

- **<u>Be curious.</u>** Curiosity creates a passion to listen. If we already know it all, we will never learn anything new. We should have a desire to grow and learn new things every day. If you continue to learn, you will not grow old.

- **<u>Be humble.</u>** Humility sensitizes our ability to listen, whereas pride dulls our ability to hear.
- **<u>Be teachable.</u>** Realize that others - no matter how we see them - can teach us something. Look for a lesson in every encounter.

Try to understand what they are saying.

Try to understand what they are feeling.

Try to understand them in this way and you will be showing them great love. You will probably eliminate a lot of arguments.

You should understand that the way you listen to your spouse, employer, teacher, colleague, friends, and children, is also the way you will listen to God!

Chapter 16 - Love is Humility

"God resists the proud,

But gives grace to the humble."[62]

Our purpose in life is not simply to know about God, but to be in communion with Him. Communion with God demands humility, because without humility how will you acknowledge that the purpose of your life is outside yourself and is in God. So long as man lives egocentrically, anthropocentrically, and autonomously, he places himself at the center and purpose of his own life. He believes that he can be perfected by his own efforts and defined by his own efforts. This is the spirit of contemporary civilization, contemporary philosophy, and contemporary politics; to create an even better world with man as its center and no reference to God and no acknowledgement that God is the source of all good.

This is the fault that Adam committed, believing that with only his own powers he could become as God, that he could complete himself. The fault of Adam is one that all humanistic creeds make. Throughout all the ages they do not consider that communion with God is indispensable for the completion of man

Humility is the antidote for this pride.

God calls us to humbly bow down to Him, with a sense of submission. There is a fine line between humility and arrogance. Humility is an attitude of the heart. The opposite of pride. God hates pride. To walk humbly with God is to recognize our relationship and to acknowledge its importance and priority in our life. It is to recognize His greatness and our lowliness.

He has shown you, O man, what is good; And what does the Lord require of you But to do justly, To love mercy, And to walk humbly with your God? [Micah 6:8 (NKJV)]

When you genuinely love another, you subjugate your needs for their pleasure.

Is this a healthy attitude?

Certainly, but if taken too far, it can be detrimental to your own health. In my book, "Physician, Heal Thyself" I pointed out that your ability to help others will be negatively impacted if you are not taking care of yourself. When one is not healthy, physically, emotionally, or spiritually, they cannot adequately help others.

This is true for medical professionals, spiritual leaders, caregivers, and anyone who desires to give of their love. In the context of this book, the ability to show love for another must be based on a healthy self-love, which originates from being loved by our Creator. Remember the biblical mandate is to *love your neighbor as yourself.* If you cannot love yourself, then you are not ready to love another successfully and in true humility.

When you attempt to fake humility, it comes across as pride.

Adam and Eve walked humbly with God before the enemy convinced them they could be as God.

Gen. 3:8 (NKJV) And they heard the sound of the Lord God walking in the garden in the cool of the day, and Adam and his wife hid themselves from the presence of the Lord God among the trees of the garden.

God does not want us to hide from Him, but to enter His presence and allow Him to change us. Enoch[63] who walked humbly with God, did not die. He had such an intimate relationship with God that God caught him up into heaven.

Noah walked humbly with God[64]. God's original plan and purpose for humankind was to walk with Him in Paradise, in His glorious presence, but sin brought the separation between God and man. Jesus 'death and resurrection made the way to the restoration of that intimate spiritual walk. We need to rest in God's presence, to enter His peace.

Humility is a factor in how we listen and respond to someone.

Romans 12:15-17 "Rejoice with those who rejoice, and weep with those who weep. Be of the same mind toward one another. Do not set your mind on high things, but associate with the humble. Do not be wise in your own opinion. Repay no one evil for evil. Have regard for good things in the sight of all men."

Humility sensitizes our hearing, whereas pride dulls our ability to hear. How do you listen to your spouse, employer/supervisor, colleagues, friends, or your children?

It was just before the feast of Passover and Jesus knew that His hour had come. This was the point in time for which He had come into this world. There had been earlier days when Jesus had said that His hour was not yet[65], but the time had come, this was day that was anticipated. His public ministry is over, within twenty-four hours He would be crucified. It was the beginning of the end, and Jesus would use these last precious hours to convey to His disciples how He genuinely loved them. For three years, He led them, taught them, cared for them, and protected them. He had given them more than any other leader could ever give his followers.

After the evening meal, Jesus did something so astonishing as it broke all the rules of propriety in that culture, and demonstrated His love for them, and in so doing, taught a valuable lesson in showing love.

Jesus will lower Himself, literally stooping in humble service to His disciples. But as He serves in this humble way, He does not do it from weakness. He does it from a position of authority. Jesus knew His authority and knew His relationship with God the Father. He knew His identity, as the one who had come from God, and was going back to God.

It was the custom for the lowest servant of the house to wash the feet of guests as they entered the house. For some reason, no one had done this when Jesus and the disciples came into the room. So, they ate their meal with dirty feet. How awkward was this? First, because of the sandals they wore and the roads on which they walked; their feet would be dirty.

Second, the disciples would eat a formal meal like this at a table known as a triclinium. This was a low (coffee-table height), U-shaped table. Guests would sit, and their status at the meal was reflected by how close they were seated to the host or leader of the meal. Because the table was low, they did not sit on chairs. They leaned on pillows, with their feet behind them. This meant that dirty feet could be unpleasantly close to the table during the meal. So, the unwashed feet were conspicuous.

So why didn't any of the disciples do this first? Any disciple would have gladly washed Jesus' feet. but they could not wash His without having to be available to wash the others, and that would have been an intolerable admission of inferiority among their fellows. So, no one's feet got washed!

Jesus essentially acted out a parable for the disciples - actions speak louder than words. So, when He wanted to teach the proud, arguing disciples about true love, He took on the task of the lowest servant in the household. He began to wash the feet of His disciples.

At this critical moment, the evening before the torture of the cross, Jesus rises from the table, laid aside His clothes, picked up a towel and girded Himself. He then filled a basin with water and began to wash their feet. This was an extreme act of servanthood. Jesus went around the table, washing and drying the feet of His disciples. You should take note that this occurred right after the disciples had argued over who would be the greatest in the Kingdom.[66]

Here Jesus illustrates what makes true greatness, "*He that would be the greatest let him be the servant of all.*"

Peter objects to Jesus washing his feet.

"Lord, are you going to wash my feet?"

Jesus replied, "*You do not realize now what I am doing, but later you will understand."*

"No," said Peter, *"You shall never wash my feet."*

Jesus answered, *"Unless I wash you, you have no part with me."*

Peter was probably seated at the far end of the table from Jesus and He may have come to Peter last of all and he clearly felt uncomfortable with Jesus performing such a humble act of service for him. It is difficult for some to receive loving acts of kindness from others.

After Jesus washes the feet of the apostles, He explains and charges them.

> *You call me Teacher and Lord, and you say well, for so I am. If I then, your Lord and Teacher, have washed your feet, you also ought to wash one another's feet. For I have given you an example, that you should do as I have done to you. Most assuredly, I say to you, a servant is not greater than his master; nor is he who is sent greater than he who sent him. If you know these things, blessed are you if you do them.*

[John 13:13-17 (NKJV)]

By inference, that is also what Jesus is calling us to do.

C. S. Lewis writes.

> *There is one vice of which no man in the world is free; which everyone in the world loathes when he sees it in someone else and of which hardly any people except Christians ever imagine*

they are guilty of themselves. ...... the more we have it, the more we dislike it in others. Pride or self-conceit. .... It was pride that made Satan become Satan..... It is the complete anti-God state of mind.

It was Satan who through Eve's pride convinced her she could be as God if she ate from the Tree of Knowledge...

It was with pride that Cain presented his good works to God in place of a blood sacrifice.

Judas, through pride believed he could change things by betraying Jesus.

The antidote to pride is humility.

Philippians 2:5-8 (NKJV) Let this mind be in you which was also in Christ Jesus, who, being in the form of God, did not consider it robbery to be equal with God, but made Himself of no reputation, taking the form of a bondservant, and coming in the likeness of men. And being found in appearance as a man, He humbled Himself and became obedient to the point of death, even the death of the cross.

Humility is not developing a low opinion of self; true humility is knowing yourself and not trying to become something or someone you are not.

Therefore, whoever humbles himself as this little child is the greatest in the kingdom of heaven. [Matthew 18:4 (NKJV)]

Proverbs 11:2 (NKJV) When pride comes, then comes shame; But with the humble is wisdom.

In unity with humility it is not possible that there should be any sign of malice, or of any argument, or even the smell of disobedience, unless faith is the matter of dispute. He who has as a bride humility, is before everything else meek, mild, full of remorse, sympathetic, concerned, radiant, pliable, not offensive, alert, not lazy, and why say any more?

He is free from passion, for the Lord recalled us in our humility, and delivered us from all our enemies, and our passions and corruptions.[67]

Chapter 17 – Love is Forgiving

We first met Thomasine Crowe and her husband, Bobby, on a mission trip to Costa Rica in 1994. Six years later she shared her testimony at the church we pastored. Her testimony shows what is possible when anger and bitterness are laid down and forgiveness takes over.

In 1987 Thomasine's 26-year-old son was brutally murdered during a robbery by the son of a pastor. She was angry and bitter toward God and the murderer. It ate at her day and night until a couple in her Louisiana church encouraged her to forgive for her own healing. Thomasine eventually made the decision to forgive her son's murderer. Later she went to visit him in prison to tell him of her forgiveness. They began to correspond, and she visited him again. As a result of Thomasine's forgiveness, Ricky Blackmon was able to receive the forgiveness of Jesus Christ. His sins were forgiven, but there were still consequences to his crime. On August 5, 1999, with Thomasine in attendance, Ricky Blackmon was executed.[44]

Thomasine became active in an organization ministering to crime victims and their families, teaching them the need to forgive.

How can we forgive the person that hurt us deeply?

Forgiving someone who has hurt you does not relieve them of the consequences of their acts, it is for your benefit, not theirs. Your forgiveness frees you from bondage to that hurt.

The first step in forgiving others is to admit that we are also sinners. We get so caught up with what has been done to us that we ignore the fact that we are far from perfect. Jesus went to the cross to forgive the sins of the world, but before the cross there was the Garden of Gethsemane. It was there that Jesus fell on His knees before the Father, humbled Himself and said, "Not my will, but Your will be done.[45]"

He laid aside His desires and opened Himself up to do the will of His Father. Before we take our hurt to the cross and forgive others, we must look at ourselves and check our motivation. Gethsemane is the place where Jesus, in prayer, laid aside His righteousness and became all that we are. We must lay aside our self-righteousness.

We need to pray, *"Lord, show me my sin, and identify me with the sin of all mankind."*

If we do not lose our self-righteousness, we will never be free of the hurt.We will just keep on wearing our martyr hat and saying, *"We forgave them, why does it still hurt?"*

Our forgiveness is not complete until we get down off our exalted position. A good way to begin our prayer to forgive is, "Lord, take me to Gethsemane with You until all those lines of who is right and who is wrong are lost in the sense of common shame at the foot of the cross."

The second step in forgiving someone's injustice to us is to receive our own forgiveness. Forgiveness is impossible in our human flesh. We cannot even forgive ourselves. Only Jesus can enter our heart and change it. We must be able to receive God's gift of forgiveness. Then forgiving others can be simple. When we come through Gethsemane, we know that neither the one who hurt us nor ourselves truly deserve to be forgiven. But through Jesus Christ, we can forgive the one who caused us harm.

The third step is harder yet. More than forgiveness is required. We are commanded to bless those who hurt us[46]. That means we are to pray for all manner of good things to happen to them. Bless them, rejoice with them, and mourn with them. If he is hungry, feed him; if he is thirsty, give him something to drink.[47]

Chapter 18 - Seek First the Kingdom of God

But seek the kingdom of God, and all these things shall be
added to you.
[Luke 12:31 (NKJV)]

Ever since I can remember, I have been a foodie, a collector of restaurants, in my mind if not in reality.

In my previous life, traveling was part of my job description and dining on an expense account was a perk. The places I remember most are the ones with the best food, service, and atmosphere. For instance, in New York City, Keene's London Chop House served a calves liver steak that was out of this world, but after dinner I could call for tobacco and my churchwarden pipe, which hung from the ceiling along with the many thousands. The Longfellow House in Pascagoula, MS where the poet presumably wrote some of his best stuff served a crab au gratin you would die for. Who says you do not mix cheese with seafood? Then there was: The She-Crab soup at the Kitty Knight House on Maryland's Eastern Shore; Prime Rib and strawberry shortcake at Boston's Durgin Park; pompano en papillote at Antoine's and Eggs Hussarde for breakfast at Brennan's in New Orleans. There are many other places and dinners I could name, but there is one place where the setting was so awesome, that I do not even remember the food, although I know it was also great.

A couple of miles inland from Kaneohe Bay on the windward side of Hawaii's island of Oahu, across the Mountain from Honolulu, lies the Haiku Gardens and its restaurant, Haleiwa Joe's. As we entered on my first visit, the hostess led us around a huge salad bar - with all manner of tropical fruits and salad fixings - then out onto the lanai where our table overlooked the gardens below and the mountains in the distance.

As we sat down at our table we were welcomed by swarms of myna birds looking for crumbs under the table.

Below us, the gardener had piled grass clippings in one corner of the clearing waiting to be burned. To the right of the grass pile was a small pond. In the center of the pond stood a gazebo. A narrow foot bridge allowed people to walk out to the gazebo.

There was to be a wedding that night in the gazebo, and we had a ring-side seat.

It was as if I had landed in the Garden of Eden. The following scripture came to my mind.

> *Then Jesus said to his disciples: "Therefore I tell you, do not worry about your life, what you will eat; or about your body, what you will wear. Life is more than food, and the body more than clothes. Consider the [MYNAH's]: They do not sow or reap, they have no storeroom or barn; yet God feeds them. And how much more valuable you are than birds! Who of you by worrying can add a single hour to his life? Since you cannot do this very little thing, why do you worry about the rest?*[68]

Jesus prescribes the proper attitude of His followers. It is a warning against worry. He tells them not to worry about their life.

Is this possible? Fear and worry are intricately connected. When we are afraid that our needs will not be met, we worry. When we are not in control we worry. We worry that we will not be loved.

Worry is a fear that we will never have enough.

Jesus gives us a loving command, "Do not worry!"

We often fail to appreciate what damage worry does in our lives. Research clearly shows that stress deteriorates our immune systems; people under constant or high stress show lower T-cell counts, essential for immune response. Stress has a definite effect on fertility. Prolonged stress has been shown to affect the brain, It makes a person less able to respond to future stress. And stress also is related to sudden heart failure.

We do not have to point out that these are stressful times in our nation and in the world. Everyone feels stressed from time to time. Over half of all Americans say they feel stressed out at least once a week. Only 10% say they never feel stressed.

Those mynas, picking up crumbs under my table at Haleiwa Joe's, do not worry where their next meal is coming from. God sees to it that they have food. If the restaurant closed, they would go back to feeding off the plants and trees in the jungle below.

Jesus is not frivolously telling us, "don't worry, be happy." The same can be said the term "hakuna matata," from "The Lion King," meaning "No worries."

Worry does not stop because we close our eyes to our circumstances, but because we know a loving God Who is greater than all our needs.

Worry is completely counter-productive – the stress it brings in our life does nothing but destroy.

Trusting in God does make sense. If He takes such good care of the birds, flowers, and grass, won't He also take care of us, His children? Worry cannot make you live longer, and worry can't make you any taller. If it is futile to worry about small things that are out of our control, it is even more futile to worry about big things even further out of our control.

Instead of worrying, Jesus wants us to have a child-like faith in Him.

God cares for the flowers, but that means that every day for the flowers is not sun and sweetness. If every day were sunny, and there was never clouds and rain, the flowers would die quickly. God's intention is that your attention be on His kingdom and His treasure, not the kingdom and treasure of this world.

*"Do not be afraid, little flock, for your Father has been pleased
to give you the kingdom. Sell your possessions and give to the
poor. Provide purses for yourselves that will not wear out, a
treasure in heaven that will not be exhausted, where no thief
comes near and no moth destroys. For where your treasure is,
there your heart will be also.*

Do not have an anxious mind: Jesus' good news is simple; you do
not have to hold on to the things of this world with a death grip. But
seek the kingdom of God, and all these things shall be added to you.
God wants us to be more focused on Him than on these necessities of
daily life; when we seek Him first, all the other things are added unto
us. We have sometimes thought that the only way to seek the kingdom
of God is to put away every other pursuit and go to some monastery or
desert cave. But we can seek God in what we do every day; you can seek
God at your job if you work unto the Lord and His glory. For where
your treasure is, there your heart will be also: The correlation between
where your heart is and where your treasure is isn't a suggestion; it is
a simple fact. If you regard your material possessions as your treasure,
then your heart is set here on this earth.

How can we ignore all the worries and seek His kingdom? Do not
hold on to any physical thing too tightly, hold on to eternal things.
Believe that He loves you and wants you to have the very best. Jesus let
go of everything heaven itself held and was happy with a simple trust in
His Father.

A kingdom is not always a place. The Greek term "basilea,"
translated as kingdom, can mean either realm or reign. A realm is a
geographical area over which a king reigns as in the Biblical kingdom
of Judea. It is the nation over which a king reigns and has geographical
boundaries. Reign refers to rule. It can be a time in which a sovereign
rules or a people over whom he rules.

Unfortunately, "basilea" can be translated as either reign or realm. If we look at an earthly kingdom, we can better understand a kingdom. The United Kingdom is a realm - an area controlled by the sovereign. It includes Great Britain, Scotland, Wales, and Ireland. Citizens of this realm are the subjects of the king (or queen) even when they are outside of their home country. They are the people over whom the king exercises his authority or reigns. An American citizen in England must obey the laws of the kingdom, but he is not subject to the Queen. An Englishman in America is still a subject of the reigning King or Queen.

The Kingdom of God is not heaven, although heaven is a part of that kingdom. The kingdom of God is not the church, although it could be. The Kingdom of God is wherever God rules. The Kingdom of God is not a place, the Kingdom of God is an activity. It is the activity of God ruling. Obviously, in heaven all things are ruled by God, but here on earth, there are people that have no regard for God or His rule.

If the Kingdom of God is within you[69], God is ruling and you are free to Truly love God, yourself, and others.

Do not worry if you will ever find love.

Seek first God's kingdom and you will definitely find pure, genuine, fulfilling love that will never fail you.

—The End—

If you enjoyed "Love Like Jesus," please go to your bookstore and leave a review. This will not only help the author but it will help other readers to find a book that will help them.

You can also pick up a free book on Spiritual Gifts at our our website.[1]

Did you love *Love Like Jesus*?

Then you should read "Pray Like Jesus,"[2] also by William F Johnson!

[3]

Pray and move mountains. Your prayers can change your life and move the mountains that you and others face.

Award-winning author William F. Johnson reveals the keys to effective prayer as he weaves Gospel accounts of Jesus' teachings, prayer

---

1. http://aslanpress.com

2. http://www.aslanpress.com/pray-like-jesus.html

3. http://www.aslanpress.com/pray-like-jesus.html

life, and perspectives with a personal search for more prayer effectiveness.

Follow Jesus as He reveals when, where and how to pray, Learn Jesus' perspectives on love, power, and the spiritual realm and how that affects His prayers. Several of Jesus' prayers are analyzed to uncover more insight in praying with power.

Let Jesus be your mentor as you seek a deeper prayer life.

Readers of "Pray Like Jesus" have commented:

***** *"This book is wonderful …. it has helped my prayer life and walk with Jesus. I have read it and re read many parts. it is marked up, and highlighted and will be on my most favorite list of books for many years to come… WELL DONE Bill…you really did an awesome job in writing this book… may we all learn to PRAY LIKE JESUS……"*

***** *"This was just what I was looking for. It helped me to understand the trinity better and confirmed what I already believed about our relationship with God. It helped me want to draw closer to God. I love the way it's written, and I highly recommend you read it."*

***** *"This an amazing book on prayer. It breaks down how to pray and why we pray. It is one of the best books I have read on prayer and highly recommend it. You will not be disappointed."*

Your life will be transformed as Jesus mentors you in your approach to powerful prayer.

About the Author

William (Bill) Johnson and his wife Rita live in Broken Arrow, Oklahoma and have been happily married for over fifty years. They have been in ministry together since 1980 and have taught classes and workshops throughout the US and overseas. During his time as a pastor, Bill was often called to minister to other pastors and church leaders.

In 2001, Bill & Rita, along with some friends, founded Aslan Ministries, Inc., a non-profit corporation with the purpose of encouraging and equipping the church and its leaders. Aslan Ministries Inc. provides counseling, coaching and in-person workshops on discipleship, ministry, prayer, leadership, and spiritual development. Bill began writing in elementary school and has continued throughout his career in industry before entering the ministry.

Bill's writing combines personal story and his unique insight with an orthodox Christian theology in an easy to read style that explains life issues.

Read more at William F Johnson's website[1]

[1] 1 Corinthians 11:1.

[3] Maslov, Abraham, "Theory of Human Motivation" 1943

[4] Mark 12:30

[6] Grant Ph.D., Adam M., Give and Take: Why Helping Others Drives Our Success (p. 5). Penguin Publishing Group. Kindle Edition.

[7] 1 Corinthians 13:4-8 (NKJV)

[8] Expositor's Bible Commentary, The - The Expositor's Bible Commentary – Volume 11:

[9] Romans 5:8

[10] Cook, Jerry. Love, Acceptance, and Forgiveness: Being Christian in a Non-Christian World (p. 14). Baker Publishing Group. Kindle Edition.

[11] 1 Corinthians 13:13 (NKJV)

[12] John 17:26

[13] 2 John4:8

[14] Papavassiliou, Vassilios. Thirty Steps to Heaven (Kindle Locations 2507-2511). Ancient Faith Publishing. Kindle Edition.

[15] The Ladder of Devine Ascent, St John Climacus

[16] Climacus, John. The Ladder of Divine Ascent

[17] Luke 24:49

[18] Isaiah 44:3: Joel 2:28-30; Ezekiel 36:25-28

[19] Ephesians 1:18-19

[20] Jn.4:24.

[21] Jn 1:18

[22] Jn14:6

[23] R.T. Kendall. Sensitivity Of The Holy Spirit: Learning to stay in the flow of God's direction, Charisma House, Lake Mary FL 2002

[24] Matthew 10:16

[25] Ephesians 4:30

[26] 1 Thessalonians 5:19

[27] Acts 1:5,

[28] Ephesians 3:19

[29] Mark 1:9-11

[30] J. I. Packer, "Knowing God" Intervarsity Press, Downers Grove, IL, 1973

[31] Wolfe, Thomas, You Can't Go Home Again, Harper Perennial, 1998

[32] John 17:26

[33] Hebrews 5:8

[34] Cross Current, Desert Streams ministries, Kansas City

[35] 1 John 1:9

[36] 1 John 3:16 (NKJV)

[37] Luke 10:25-42

[38] Luke 10:36 (NASB)

[39] Steve Sjogren, Conspiracy of Kindness, Bethany House, Bloomington, MN 2993, 2003

[40] Williams, Margery, *The Velveteen Rabbit,* George H Doran Company, United Kingdom, 1922

[41] Pastor, author of many books and Founder of Elijah House Ministries with his wife Paula

[42] Fear of Vulnerability and Learning to Trust Again, Lisa Fritscher, Verywell Mind, June 25, 2020, https://www.verywellmind.com/

[43] 2 Corinthians 6:11-14 (NKJV)

[48] Bishop's Kairon, Antiochian Orthodox Church of North America

[49] Postrel, Virginia, The Future and its Enemies, the Growing Conflict Over Creativity, Enterprise, And Progress, The Free Press, Div. of Simon & Schuster, NY, NY 1998

[50] A. W. Tozier, Of God and Men - Moody Publishers / 2015

[51] Luke 22:31-32

[52] Roland Allen, The Spontaneous Expansion of The Church And the Causes which Hinder It, The Lutterworth Press, Cambridge 1960, first published in 1927

[53] music by Jerome Kern and lyrics by Dorothy Fields From the Movie "Swing Time" with Fred Astaire & Ginger Rogers

[54] Sweet, Leonard, "Viral How Social Networking is Poised to Ignite Revival" Waterbrook Press, Colorado Springs, Co 2012

[55] Daniel 12:4 (NKJV)

[56] *Pascal, Blaise, Pascal's Penses*

[57] John 17:23

[58] Romans 8:16

[59] Hebrews 11:6

[60] Romans 8:15 (NKJV)

[61]https://www.statista.com/statistics/252393/total-us-expenditure-for-mental-health-services/

[62] James 4:6 (NKJV)

[63] Gen. 5:24

[64] Gen. 6:9

[65] John 7:30; 8:20

[66] Luke 22:23

[67] Climacus, John. The Ladder of Divine Ascent (p. 105). Kindle Edition.

[44] Michael Graczyk, Associated Press, Laredo Morning Times, August 5, 1999, P4a

[45] Luke 22:42

[46] 1 Peter 3:9

[47] Romans 12:14-21

[68] Luke 12:22-32.

[69] Luke 17L21

Don't miss out!

Visit the website below and you can sign up to receive emails whenever William F Johnson publishes a new book. There's no charge and no obligation.

https://books2read.com/r/B-A-DFXI-GPTJB

BOOKS2READ

Connecting independent readers to independent writers.

Did you love *Love Like Jesus*? Then you should read *Pray Like Jesus*[2] by William F Johnson!

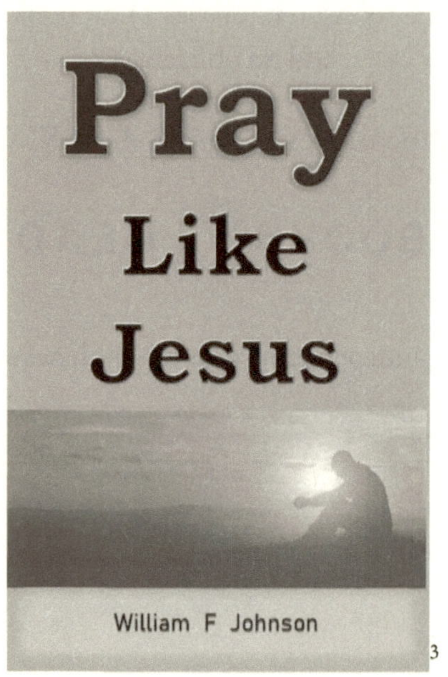

[3]

Pray and move mountains

Your prayers can change your life, your surroundings, and the world in which you live..

Discover your keys to powerful prayer.

Award-winning author William F. Johnson reveals the keys to effective prayer as he weaves Gospel accounts of Jesus' teachings, prayer life, and perspectives with a personal search for more prayer effectiveness.

Follow Jesus as He reveals when, where and how to pray, Learn Jesus' perspectives on love, power, and the spiritual realm and how that

---

2. https://books2read.com/u/bQKMYP

3. https://books2read.com/u/bQKMYP

affects His prayers. Several of Jesus' prayers are analyzed to uncover more insight in praying with power.

Let Jesus be your mentor as you seek a deeper prayer life.

Readers have commented:

***** "This book is wonderful .... it has helped my prayer life and walk with Jesus. I have read it and re read many parts.. it is marked up, and high lighted and will be on my most favorite list of books for many years to come... WELL DONE Bill...you really did an awesom job in writing this book... may we all learn to PRAY LIKE JESUS......"

***** "This was just what I was looking for. It helped me to understand the trinity better and confirmed what I already believed about our relationship with God. It helped me want to draw closer to God. I love the way it's written and I highly recommend you read it."

***** "This an amazing book on prayer. It breaks down how to pray and why we pray. It is one of the best books I have read on prayer and highly recommend it. You will not be disappointed."

Your life will be transformed as Jesus mentors you in your approach to powerful prayer.

Read more at aslanpress.com.

Also by William F Johnson

The Ministry of Jesus
Heal Like Jesus
Love Like Jesus
Pray Like Jesus

Standalone
When You Pray
Leading Your Ministry to Financial Health
Built to Last
Use Your Spiritual Gifts
Destiny
Physician, Heal Thyself; The Oxygen Mask Principle
Conflict Resolution

Watch for more at aslanpress.com.

About the Author

William (Bill) Johnson and his wife Rita live in Broken Arrow, Oklahoma and have been happily married for over fifty years. They have been in ministry together since 1980 and have taught classes and workshops throughout the US and overseas. During the past years of ministry, Bill often ministered to pastors and church leaders. In 2001, Bill & Rita - along with some sympathetic friends - established Aslan Ministries, Inc. a non-profit corporation with the purpose of encouraging and equipping the church and its leaders. Aslan Ministries Inc. provides counseling, coaching and in-person workshops on discipleship, ministry, prayer, leadership, and spiritual development.

Read more at aslanpress.com.